To my dear friend,
Beverley —

remembering all the
pleasant times we've shared
with you ~ John — Delores

J0633374

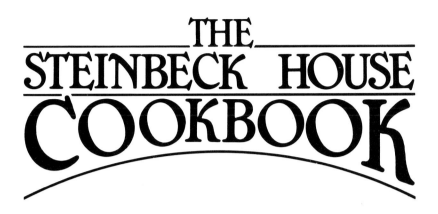

THE STEINBECK HOUSE COOKBOOK

Compiled and Published
by

THE VALLEY GUILD
of Salinas, California
Recipes edited by Kay Hillyard

1984

The Purpose of The Valley Guild

"The specific and primary purpose of The Valley Guild is to maintain and preserve the John Steinbeck House and create new revenues for charities in the Salinas Valley."

From Articles of Incorporation
October 10, 1973

Proceeds from the sale of this book will contribute to the preservation of the John Steinbeck House and provide additional revenues for charities in the Salinas Valley.

COPYRIGHT © 1984

THE VALLEY GUILD
132 Central Avenue
Salinas, California 93901

All rights reserved, including the right to reproduce this book, or parts thereof, in any form, except with the written permission of the Valley Guild.

ISBN 0-9612742-0-4
Library of Congress number: 84-50259

First Printing . . . . 10,000 copies . . . . May, 1984

Printed in USA
by
S.C. Toof & Co.
Memphis, TN

TABLE OF CONTENTS

SEEING STARS?

Every year over 18,000 happy luncheon guests at STEINBECK HOUSE applaud the cooking and beg for the recipes. So that you, too, may try, enjoy, and brag about the same tasteful entrees, soups, desserts, salads, and side dishes that have appeared on our menus throughout the years, we've given each one a special star. That doesn't mean that the other recipes aren't of star quality. They are! So much so they'll probably appear on future menus and receive their own stars. But at the moment, they are "recipes-in-waiting"—tested, tasted, and ready for stardom.

John Steinbeck, the author

PREFACE

In all his varied and eventful life, when John Steinbeck spoke of "the City," he didn't mean New York where he lived or Paris where he often visited or London which he greatly admired. He meant San Francisco. He was a man always turned toward America's West.

San Francisco was the city to which he was taken as a child to see the sights. In his youth that city provided him with his first taste of culture: Eleanora Duse acting sublimely in Ibsen's GHOSTS, Chaliapin singing BORIS GODUNOV. He savored his first independence there, living where he chose, doing as he wanted, eating at random when and where and what he liked. And he always raved about the "what."

Furthermore, he got superior food at home in Salinas in Monterey County. He was blessed with a family of good cooks who cared about the meals they served. So no wonder he always said the cuisine of Northern California was the best.

As he became celebrated and traveled the world, he developed what the French call "le bec fin," a discriminating palate. He learned to appreciate all kinds of food: the spicy dishes of Mexico, the subtle sauces of France, the infinite variety of Italy, and the complex table of the Orient. But when it came right down to it, he always longed for the food of his homeland.

The fish from that sea was the freshest, the vegetables and fruits unparalleled in this world, the very bread was life-giving. And given these abundant glories of produce, of course they should always be prepared and served in the style of San Francisco and Monterey County.

Whenever I lunch at the Steinbeck House in Salinas, I feel the spirit of John beside me. He would love the ambience of the house, his boyhood home recreated by the devoted and talented women of the Valley Guild. He would love the company of his fellow Californians. And surely he would love the food upon the table.

"Get the recipes for these wonderful dishes," he would undoubtedly urge me. "Let's make them at home in New York and Sag Harbor."

All of us in the Steinbeck family hope you will enjoy the recipes in this book and make them in your home.

Elaine Steinbeck
(Mrs. John Steinbeck)

ACKNOWLEDGMENTS

We are deeply grateful to the following people for their help in making this book an actuality:

Mrs. E. G. (Beth) Ainsworth, Mrs. John (Elaine) Steinbeck, Mrs. C. J. (Esther) Rogers, Steve Crouch, Ethlyn Crouch, E. Arlyle Grensted, Lee Richard Hayman, La Verta Zarnowski, Gary Moore, Eleanor Perry, and all the members of the Valley Guild.

PHOTOGRAPHY

Color photographs. . . . . .Steve Crouch
Black and white photographs. . . . . .E. Arlyle Grensted

FOREWORD

Since the writings of John Steinbeck, more than those of any other American author of this century, have been woven into the very fabric of our culture, it is not surprising that his talent includes the creation of his own recipes and affectionate attention to the enjoyment of the bounty of California's fields and ocean.

Steinbeck's genius for creating mood and evoking sensory response to the pleasures of eating is beautifully demonstrated in the vignette "Breakfast," one of THE LONG VALLEY stories, later included as part of chapter twenty-two in THE GRAPES OF WRATH. The sketch is a classic evocation of the smells, tastes, and warmth of a relaxed, hearty breakfast shared by the best of folk. Linda Wolfe uses the short piece to conclude her book, THE LITERARY GOURMET, one of numerous anthologies that include this gem of description.

Many memorable references to food and drink appear in Steinbeck's stories and novels. "The marvelous texture of their tortillas" is the pride of the Lopez sisters in THE PASTURES OF HEAVEN, and mouth-watering mention of other tortillas is made in "Flight" and in THE PEARL. Lee's mysterious "almost black liquor", ng-ka-py, tastes of "good rotten apples" in EAST OF EDEN and makes the reader wonder what exotic ingredients the Oriental drink might contain. The meals in TORTILLA FLAT are not always of gourmet quality, but Danny's final party includes enticing "basins of rice, pots of steaming chicken, dumplings to startle you."

In CANNERY ROW Doc downs a day's fare that might give pause to even the most adventurous diners. On his way from Monterey to La Jolla he stops for a hamburger in Gonzales, in King City, and again in Paso Robles; then he has two hamburgers and a beer in Santa Maria. In Santa Barbara he partakes of soup, lettuce and string bean salad, pot roast and mashed potatoes, and the day's first order of pineapple pie and blue cheese, plus coffee. Farther down the coast, in Carpenteria, he has only a cheese sandwich, and in Ventura he orders his now-famous beer milk shake. That evening in Los Angeles his dinner is fried chicken, julienne potatoes, hot biscuits and honey, and the day's second helping of pineapple pie and blue cheese. His has to be one of contemporary literature's heartiest appetites.

For Steinbeck, a heated can of beans represents the easiest path to "convenience foods." Dr. Phillips prepares such a hurried lunch in the often anthologized story "The Snake," and George and Lennie sup on canned beans the evening before they reach their Soledad ranch in OF MICE AND MEN. (Lennie, of course, longs for ketchup on his beans, but they "ain't got any.")

Steinbeck authored at least one published recipe. It appears in the two different editions of FAMOUS RECIPES BY FAMOUS PEOPLE, edited by Herbert Cerwin. The earlier edition titles the recipe "Tortilla Flat" and the later edition renames it "Of Beef and Men." The recipe calls for soaking the beef four hours in vinegar before draining and cooking it in a large casserole with a can of tomato sauce and one of mushrooms, then adding a cup of rich cream after the casserole is removed from the oven.

For Dean Faulkner Wells' THE GREAT AMERICAN WRITERS' COOKBOOK Elaine Steinbeck has contributed John's favorite fish recipe, "Mysterious Striped Bass." After the bass is beheaded, skinned and filleted, it is sprinkled with lemon juice and refrigerated. When the moment of truth is at hand, the fish is placed in a shallow, buttered pan, sprinkled with salt and pepper, melted butter, lemon juice, and dried minced onions, put under a broiler pre-heated to high and cooked until lightly brown. At that point more melted butter is added, if needed, plus three ounces of gin; the pan is then put back under the broiler, for a flambé effect, until the bass is brown.

Another fish recipe, known on Cannery Row in Monterey as "Steinbeck Salmon," is recalled by Alicia Harby de Noon, proprietor of the famed establishment that was Lee Chong's grocery, immortalized in CANNERY ROW and SWEET THURSDAY. The top of the salmon is skinned and punctured with ten holes into which are stuffed fresh chopped parsley, garlic, Italian seasoning, and celery seed. Then the fish is rubbed lightly with olive oil, sprinkled with salt and lemon pepper, and baked. Steinbeck, an enthusiastic fisherman, would certainly approve!

John Steinbeck's writing has richly influenced American music, art, theater, film, and literature; and so it should come as no surprise that his genius extends into the world of preparing food for the adventure and pleasure of us "the people."

— Lee Richard Hayman

INTRODUCTION

Far too many beautiful and historic turn-of-the-century houses in this country have been torn down in the name of progress. Frequently such destruction of our architectural heritage is regretted too late. The farsighted Valley Guild is the civic-minded organization responsible for preserving what must be one of the most important homes in Salinas—the Steinbeck House.

Built in 1897 by J. J. Conner in what was then a prestigious residential area, the late Victorian house is now a part of the oldest section of that central coast California city. The fifteen rooms of the two-story frame structure have been refurbished to create a feeling of the Steinbeck family's presence.

The reception room to the left of the entrance was the master bedroom of Steinbeck's parents after they purchase the house in 1900. John Steinbeck was delivered there by Dr. Henry Murphy on February 27, 1902. During his high school years, when young John first began writing short stories, his bedroom was directly above his birthplace. This second floor room had previously been part of the attic play area used by him and his three sisters, Esther, Elizabeth, and Mary.

The house, located on the corner of Central Avenue and Stone Street, is described in Steinbeck's family saga, *EAST OF EDEN*, as "an immaculate and friendly house, grand enough but not pretentious, and it sat inside its white fence, surrounded by its clipped lawn, and roses and cotoneasters lapped against its white walls."

After John's parents died in the mid-1930's, the Klute family purchased and lived in the house until 1953. Later it was bequeathed to the Sacred Heart Parish, which used the building as a student center for the Newman Club of Hartnell College until 1971.

In the fall of that year, the Valley Guild was organized by four Salinas Valley women who envisioned launching a luncheon restaurant which would offer the best of the area's fresh vegetables and fruits as they came into season. Their plan was to staff the operation with volunteers who would rotate their services on a flexible schedule. All proceeds would first cover expenses, and remaining profits would be distributed to various charities in the Valley.

By the spring of 1972 the nucleus of the Valley Guild had been augmented with the enthusiastic participation of ten more women interested in good food and volunteer service for a worthy project in their community. It was then that the group learned that the Steinbeck House was being offered for sale and began negotiations for its purchase. With only two months allowed for the raising of a $56,000 cash payment, the Guild quickly recruited sixty-seven new members to assist in a fund-raising drive that collected more than $100,000 in a mere forty-nine days.

The acquisition of the building was just the beginning of the Guild's work, however. Thorough renovation, appropriate redecorating and tasteful furnishing had to be undertaken—and were, with great zeal.

The grand opening of the Steinbeck House Restaurant took place on February 27, 1974, the seventy-second anniversary of the Nobel laureate's birth. The following year the Guild opened The Best Cellar, its basement gift shop, and created an additional source of income. Combined profits from the restaurant and the gift shop have, to date, netted more than $200,000 for local charities.

Today the two seatings for gourmet lunches (including many creations from recipes in this book) are offered five days a week and require reservations well in advance because of the continuing popularity among Salinas Valley patrons as well as visitors from all over the world.

The adventure of eating in the house where America's perennially popular author was born and grew up is a memorable highlight for hundreds of tourists each year. And contributing to this pleasurable experience is the contagious feeling of goodwill, enthusiasm for and appreciation of the Long Valley that emanates from the volunteer ladies who operate the Steinbeck House so successfully. Dressed in their Victorian attire, they create an ambience of warm friendliness and convivial enjoyment in their work that would make the original Steinbeck family residents mightily pleased that their home has been preserved so hospitably.

— *Lee Richard Hayman*

Steinbeck
Family
Photos

John on the steps of the front porch

John's sister Mary, and John on "Jill," John's own red pony

John's sister, Esther

John's sister, Beth

John on the front lawn

John with his dog

The family in the living room, Christmas Day, 1919
John, mother, sister Mary, father

16

The living room today

©Steve Crouch

Appetizers, Cocktails and Wines

At Steinbeck House light wine cocktails are served, Cannery Row and Wine Cooler being two of the most popular. Recipes in this section also include various appetizers—dips, vegetables, pâtés, canapés—to accompany luncheon drinks.

MINIATURE STRUDELS

Makes: 80 small strudels
Temperature: 350°
Baking time: 15 minutes
Cookie sheets

This dough is very easy to handle.

PASTRY
1 stick butter
1 cup sour cream
2 egg yolks
2 cups sifted flour

1. Melt butter in a medium saucepan over low heat. With a spoon slowly beat in sour cream.
2. Stir in egg yolks; then add the flour and stir until well blended. Remove from heat.
3. Shape mixture into ¾ inch balls and refrigerate in single layer in shallow dish; cover tightly, chill overnight.

FILLING
1 pound Gouda cheese, grated
½ cup finely chopped pecans
Black pepper to taste
Nutmeg to taste

TO ASSEMBLE:
1. Mix cheese with pecans and seasonings.
2. Roll pastry balls into 4 inch rounds.
3. Place a teaspoonful of cheese mixture in center of each round. Bring opposite sides of dough rounds to center and pinch edges together making a seam down the middle. Tuck each end under to seal.
4. Place on lightly greased cookie sheets. Bake at 350° for 15 minutes or until lightly browned.
5. Remove to serving dish and dust with additional nutmeg. Serve warm.

ARTICHOKE CHILI DIP

Temperature: 350°
Baking time: 5 minutes
10 inch pie or quiche plate

1 jar (6 ounces) marinated artichoke
   hearts, partially drained
1 package (8 ounces) frozen artichoke
   hearts, cooked according to directions
1 can (4 ounces) chopped chilies
6 tablespoons mayonnaise
1$\frac{1}{2}$ cups grated Cheddar cheese

1. Finely chop both marinated and cooked artichoke hearts; spread in bottom of pie plate.
2. Drain chilies and spread over chopped artichoke hearts.
3. Cover with a thin layer of mayonnaise.
4. Sprinkle grated cheese over mayonnaise.
5. Bake at 350° for 5 minutes, or until cheese is melted.
6. Serve at once with tortilla chips.

ENGLISH CHEESE NIBBLES

Serves: 12

1 cup chopped black olives
$\frac{1}{2}$ cup thinly-sliced green onions
1$\frac{1}{2}$ cups grated mild Longhorn cheese
$\frac{1}{2}$ cup mayonnaise
$\frac{1}{2}$ teaspoon salt
$\frac{1}{4}$ teaspoon curry
6 English muffins, split

1. Mix olives, green onions, cheese, mayonnaise, and seasonings.
2. Spread on split English muffins.
3. Heat under broiler until cheese melts and bubbles lightly.
4. Cut muffins in quarters. Serve hot as an appetizer.

BUTTER BREAK-APARTS

Makes: 50
Temperature: 450°
Baking time: 15 minutes
13 x 9 x 2 inch pan

A quick and easy appetizer.

¹/₃ cup butter
2¹/₄ cups flour
1 tablespoon sugar
2¹/₂ teaspoons baking powder
1 teaspoon salt
1 cup milk

1. Heat oven to 450.° While heating, melt butter in 13 x 9 inch baking dish, right in the oven.
2. Sift flour, sugar, baking powder, and salt into large mixing bowl.
3. Select one of the seasoning variations listed below; add ingredients for #1, #2, or #3 to flour at this point.
4. Add milk and stir slowly with a fork until dough clings together (about 30 strokes).
5. Turn onto a well-floured board and roll over to coat lightly with flour; knead about 10 times.
6. Roll into a rectangle ¹/₂ inch thick and about 16 inches long and 6 inches wide. With a floured knife, cut in half lengthwise, then crosswise in ¹/₂ inch wide strips. Each strip should be about 3 inches long.
7. Dip both sides of each strip in the melted butter, then arrange in 2 rows in pan so that sides touch each other.
8. For variations #1, #2, and #4, sprinkle strips with topping.
9. Bake on middle rack of oven for 15 minutes or until golden brown. Serve hot.

VARIATIONS
1. Add ¹/₄ cup minced chives to flour mixture. Sprinkle tops with ¹/₄ cup grated Parmesan cheese before baking.
2. Add 1 clove minced garlic to flour mixture. Sprinkle tops with celery seed and paprika or garlic salt before baking.
3. Add ¹/₂ cup grated sharp Cheddar cheese to flour mixture.
4. Sprinkle tops with 3 tablespoons sugar mixed with 1 teaspoon cinnamon before baking.

BROCCOLI STICKS

Serves: 4

The broccoli must be very fresh and green for this dish.

Stems from 4 to 5 pounds of peeled broccoli
1 teaspoon chili powder
¹/₂ teaspoon lemon pepper

1. Using the heavy portion of the broccoli stems, cut into lengths of 1 to 1¹/₂ inches.
2. Combine chili powder and lemon pepper in small bowl.
3. Either serve chili powder mixture separately as a dip or arrange dipped broccoli stems on lettuce-lined platter.

    NOTE: This is a new, tasty combination and a very colorful one. Use the broccoli flowerets with the sauce for Broccoli Puffs (see page 26).

FRENCH-FRIED ARTICHOKES

Serves: 4-6
Temperature: 350°-375°
Electric fry pan

Hidden inside the crisp coating is a tender heart of artichoke.

1 egg
¹/₂ cup low-fat milk
1 teaspoon salt
¹/₂ teaspoon garlic salt
¹/₄ cup flour
³/₄ cup buttermilk baking mix
1¹/₂ teaspoons baking powder
¹/₄ cup chopped red onion
1 tablespoon chopped fresh parsley or
    dried parsley flakes
2 packages (9 ounces each) frozen
    artichokes, thawed, and well drained
Oil for frying

1. Beat egg and milk with electric beater.
2. Continue beating while adding salt, garlic salt, flour, buttermilk baking mix, and baking powder.
3. By hand, stir in chopped onion and parsley. Batter should be consistency of heavy cream.
4. Fill fry pan about ¹/₂ full of oil and heat to 350.° Coat artichokes with batter and gently drop in hot oil, a few at a time; fry until golden brown. Drain on paper towels and serve immediately.

COCONUT-CHEESE TIDBITS

Makes: 4 dozen
Temperature: 350°
Baking time: 20 minutes
Madeleine pan or 1½ inch
*   muffin pans*

2 cups sugar
½ cup water
6 eggs, slightly beaten
1 cup whole wheat flour
3 tablespoons butter
½ cup grated Parmesan cheese
1½ cups freshly grated coconut

1. Over high heat, boil sugar and water to soft-ball stage (240° on candy thermometer), stirring frequently.
2. Remove from heat and beat syrup slowly into eggs with electric hand mixer at low speed.
3. Slowly add flour, butter, cheese, and coconut and mix well.
4. Spoon batter into well-greased Madeleine pans or 1½ inch muffin tins. Bake at 350° for 20 minutes.
5. Serve warm or cold with fruit salads or desserts.

TOASTED COCONUT CHIPS

Temperature: 200°
Baking time: 1 — 1½ hours
Baking sheet

Good as an appetizer or for nibbling anytime.

1. Pierce eyes of coconut and drain off milk. Heat the nut in a 350° oven for 25 minutes. When cool, tap gently with hammer until it cracks into large pieces. Leaving brown skin intact, pry out the meat. Slice thin with a vegetable peeler.
2. Spread on a baking sheet and bake at 200° for 1 to 1½ hours, or until very crisp and lightly browned. Stir occasionally during baking.
3. Pack in airtight jars.

24

CHICKEN AND CHICKEN LIVER PÂTÉ

Makes: 5 cups pâté

1 2¹/₂- to 3-pound fryer, quartered
1 onion
3 whole cloves
1 stalk celery
1 carrot
Salt to taste
Pepper to taste
2 cups water
1 pound chicken livers
1¹/₄ cups water
2 green onions, sliced
2 cloves garlic, peeled
¹/₄ pound (1 stick) sweet butter
1 teaspoon salt
¹/₂ teaspoon seasoned salt
¹/₂ teaspoon pepper
¹/₂ teaspoon nutmeg
1 teaspoon dried parsley
¹/₂ teaspoon powdered sage
2¹/₂ tablespoons brandy
1 cup chopped pistachio nuts (or pecans)

1. Cook fryer with onion, cloves, celery, carrot, salt, pepper, and the 2 cups water in a plastic roasting bag in a 350° oven for 50 to 60 minutes. Refrigerate until cool enough to handle.

2. Drain off broth from bag and save.

3. Remove skin and bones from chicken, saving skin. Finely shred the chicken.

4. Bring chicken livers to a boil in the 1¹/₄ cups water, then reduce heat to simmer. Cover and cook 5 to 7 minutes, or until livers are just cooked through.

5. Drain, reserving broth.

6. Combine chicken broth and liver broth in saucepan and heat to boiling. Boil rapidly 10 to 15 minutes, or until liquid is reduced to about 1 cup.

7. Purée livers, green onions, and garlic in food processor, using metal blade. Add reserved chicken skin and the cup of hot broth and continue processing until smooth.

8. Add butter, salt and seasoned salt, pepper, nutmeg, parsley, sage, and brandy. Continue to process until very smooth.

9. Turn puréed mixture into a bowl and stir in the shredded chicken and ¹/₄ cup of the pistachio nuts.

10. Line a 1¹/₂-quart round bottom bowl with plastic wrap and press pâté gently into lined bowl. Refrigerate several hours (or overnight) or until firm.

11. To serve, turn out onto serving dish, remove plastic, and press remaining ³/₄ cup of pistachio nuts all over the top and sides.

12. Garnish the plate with lettuce leaves and serve with crackers or rye bread.

BROCCOLI PUFFS

Makes: 28 puffs
Deep fry at 375°

These can be made ahead and reheated in a hot oven, 425°, 8-10 minutes, uncovered.

¹/₂ cup water
¹/₄ cup (¹/₂ stick) butter
¹/₂ cup flour
2 whole eggs (large)
¹/₂ teaspoon salt
Dash of liquid hot pepper
1 cup finely chopped cooked broccoli

1. Bring water and butter to a boil. Add flour all at once and stir until mixture leaves sides of pan and forms a ball.
2. Remove from heat; add eggs, one at a time, beating well with electric mixer after each one.
3. Add seasonings, then stir in broccoli.
4. Drop by tablespoons into hot deep oil (375°) and cook until lightly browned. Drain on paper towels.

SAUCE FOR BROCCOLI PUFFS
(Makes ¹/₂ cup)
¹/₄ cup each mayonnaise and sour cream
1 teaspoon each lemon juice, creamy
    horseradish, and grated Parmesan
¹/₂ teaspoon liquid hot pepper

Mix together all ingredients and chill.

Here is an attractive new appetizer: stuffed baby brussels sprouts. With a small sharp knife, cut out the stems in tender-crisp cooked sprouts. Drain thoroughly. Fill each sprout with a half-teaspoon of deviled ham sharpened with mustard or a zesty cheese mixture. Top with a sliced, stuffed olive.

TOMATOES WITH BROCCOLI PURÉE

50 cherry tomatoes
2 cups cooked broccoli flowerets
  (1½ bunches broccoli)
1 stick butter, melted
½ teaspoon salt
¼ teaspoon black pepper
¼ teaspoon nutmeg
Dash of cayenne pepper

1. Cut off tops of tomatoes; squeeze out seeds and excess pulp; stand upside down to drain.
2. Purée flowerets in food processor or blender, slowly adding melted butter and seasonings. Taste for seasoning.
3. Spoon mixture into hollowed-out tomatoes. Arrange on a serving dish.
4. Serve as an hors d'oeuvre.
   NOTE: For good green color, you must use fresh broccoli.

CURRIED CHICKEN WINGS

Temperature: 400°
Baking time: 45 minutes
2 9 x 13-inch pans

3 pounds chicken wings
½ cup flour
2 eggs, slightly beaten
1¼ cups fine dry bread crumbs
1½ teaspoons salt
½ teaspoon pepper
2 teaspoons onion salt
2 tablespoons curry powder
⅓ cup sesame seeds
½ cup melted butter

1. Cut off and discard wing tips. Cut wings in half at joint.
2. Combine crumbs, seasonings, and sesame seeds.
3. Dip chicken in flour, then beaten eggs, then crumb mixture.
4. Arrange in single layer in 2 shallow pans (each 9 x 13 inches). Pour melted butter over chicken. Bake 45 minutes at 400° or until golden brown, turning once during baking.
5. Yields about 30 nibbles. Best served hot. This also can be used for other chicken parts.

*MARTINI   *Serves: 1*

¼ cup sake (Japanese rice wine)
1 tablespoon dry vermouth
Lemon peel
Pickled onion or stuffed olive for garnish

1. Mix sake and vermouth; chill well.
2. Rub rim of chilled glass with lemon peel.
3. Serve chilled mixture with either a pickled onion or an olive on a toothpick.

*WINE COOLER   *Serves: 1*

⅓ cup Burgundy*
⅓ cup Sprite

1. Fill a chilled 8 ounce glass with ice cubes. Pour over the Burgundy and the Sprite.

   *Chablis or Rosé may be substituted for the Burgundy.

*CANNERY ROW   *Serves: 1*

¼ cup pineapple juice
¼ cup chablis
Sprite
Maraschino cherry

1. Into chilled 8 ounce glass, half-filled with ice, pour pineapple juice and chablis.
2. Add Sprite to fill glass; garnish with a cherry.

*DAIQUIRI   *Serves: 4*

1 cup chablis
½ cup liquid Daiquiri mix
¾ teaspoon sugar
¼ teaspoon rum flavoring

1. Combine chablis, Daiquiri mix, sugar, and rum flavoring in blender. Add 2 cups crushed ice; blend till slushy.
2. Pour into icy glasses. Serve with a short straw.

*GIMLET
Serves: 4

1$\frac{1}{2}$ cups chablis
$\frac{1}{2}$ cup Rose's sweetened Lime Juice
2$\frac{1}{4}$ teaspoons sugar
$\frac{1}{2}$ cup shaved ice

1. Mix chablis, lime juice, and sugar; chill well.
2. Place a generous tablespoon of shaved ice in each chilled wine glass.
3. Fill glass with gimlet mix and serve.

*MANHATTAN
Serves: 4

$\frac{2}{3}$ cup golden sherry
2 cups sweet vermouth
3 tablespoons syrup from maraschino cherries
4 maraschino cherries

1. Mix sherry, sweet vermouth, and cherry syrup; chill well.
2. Fill each chilled wine glass with ice cubes.
3. Pour chilled Manhattan mix over ice.
4. Garnish each cocktail with maraschino cherry; serve.

KIWI DAIQUIRI
Serves: 3

$\frac{1}{2}$ to 1 ounce simple syrup (to taste)
(1 to 2 tablespoons)
4 medium kiwi fruit, peeled
Juice of $\frac{1}{2}$ medium-sized lime
1$\frac{1}{8}$ ounces (2 tablespoons plus 1 teaspoon) banana liqueur
3 ounces (6 tablespoons) light rum
2 cups crushed ice

1. Make simple syrup (1 part granulated sugar to 2 parts water; boil 5 minutes). Cool.
2. Blend kiwi, lime juice, and banana liqueur for 1 minute. Add rum, simple syrup, and ice. Blend 1 minute.
3. Serve in cold cocktail glass.

*MARGUERITA

Serves: 4

²/₃ cup sake
²/₃ cup chablis
²/₃ cup liquid sweet-and-sour mix
¹/₄ cup dry vermouth
¹/₂ cup shaved ice
2 limes
¹/₄ cup coarse salt

1. Mix sake, chablis, sweet-and-sour mix, and vermouth. Chill well for at least 2 hours or overnight.
2. Pour mixture into blender just before preparing glasses for serving.
3. Place coarse salt in flat dish.
4. Rub rim of each chilled champagne glass with cut lime. Dip rim in salt.
5. Place 1 full tablespoon of shaved ice in each glass.
6. Squeeze ¹/₃ wedge of lime over ice in each glass.
7. Blend Marguerita mixture for at least 30 seconds immediately before serving.
8. Carefully pour Marguerita mix from blender into each glass, so salted glass rim remains dry.
9. Garnish with twist of lime; serve.

CITRUS PUNCH

Makes: 28 4 ounce servings
Punch bowl

This punch is extremely easy to make in any quantity because it has so few ingredients. In addition, it is extremely thirst-quenching because it is not overly sweet.

2 cups orange juice
2 cups lemonade
2¹/₂ quarts ginger ale
Grenadine for color

1. When ready to serve, stir orange juice, lemonade, and ginger ale together.
2. Add grenadine to color.

CHAMPAGNE PUNCH

Makes: 3 quarts (24 4 ounce servings)

2 cans (6 ounces each) frozen orange juice concentrate
1 can (6 ounces) frozen lemon juice concentrate or lemonade
6 cups cold water
2½ cups ginger ale or 7-Up
1 fifth California champagne
Fresh strawberries

1. Combine orange juice concentrate, lemon juice concentrate, and water.
2. Just before serving, add ginger ale and champagne. Garnish with fresh strawberries.

CALIFORNIA SUNSHINE PUNCH

Makes: 40 5 ounce servings
Large punch bowl

This is a very refreshing wine punch.

1 large can (12 ounces) frozen lemonade
1 quart water
1 quart orange juice
1 large can (6 cups) pineapple juice
1 liter 7-Up or 1 quart ginger ale
1½ quarts chablis

1. Chill all ingredients.
2. Combine in punch bowl when ready to serve. Stir lightly.

©Steve Crouch

Breads and Muffins

Bread, a symbol of hospitality, is served with the first course at Steinbeck House. Valley Guild cooks have perfected a wide variety of recipes so that the bread enhances the menu of the day.

WHOLE WHEAT "HARD" ROLLS

Makes: 20 rolls
Temperature: 425°
Baking time: 15-20 minutes
Baking sheets

2¹/₂ cups unsifted whole wheat flour
2¹/₂ cups unsifted white flour
1 tablespoon sugar
1¹/₂ teaspoons salt
1 package (1 tablespoon) dry yeast
2 cups water
1 tablespoon butter or margarine
White of 1 egg, slightly beaten
¹/₂ teaspoon water
Additional flour if needed

1. Combine flours.

2. In large mixing bowl, thoroughly mix 2 cups of combined flours, sugar, salt, and dry yeast.

3. Combine the 2 cups water and butter in saucepan; place over low heat until liquid is very warm (120° to 130°). Gradually add to dry ingredients and beat 2 minutes at medium speed, scraping bowl occasionally.

4. Add 1 more cup combined flours and beat at high speed for 2 minutes, scraping bowl occasionally.

5. With wooden spoon stir in enough additional white flour to make a soft dough.

6. Turn dough out onto a lightly floured board; knead until smooth and elastic, about 10 minutes. Place in a greased bowl, turning to grease top. Cover; let rise in a warm place, free from draft, until double in bulk, about 1 hour.

7. Punch down dough; turn onto a lightly floured board. Divide dough in half. Divide each half into 10 equal pieces. Shape each piece into a smooth ball. Place about 3 inches apart on lightly greased baking sheets. Cover; let rise until double in bulk, about 1 hour.

8. Bake at 425° until lightly browned (about 20 minutes). Remove from oven; brush rolls with a mixture of slightly beaten egg white and water. Return to oven and bake 2 minutes longer.

9. Remove from baking sheets and cool on wire racks.

   NOTE: Rolls may be stored in plastic bags in refrigerator for a few days, or frozen for 2 months. They will become soft but, if heated at 300° for 4 to 5 minutes, will harden again.

SPRING ROLLS

Makes: 20 rolls
Temperature: 375°
Baking time: 12-15 minutes
2$\frac{1}{2}$-inch muffin pans

$\frac{1}{2}$ cup (1 stick) butter
$\frac{1}{3}$ cup whipping cream
$\frac{1}{3}$ cup sugar
$\frac{1}{3}$ teaspoon salt
$\frac{1}{2}$ teaspoon cardamom
1 package (1 tablespoon) dry yeast
$\frac{1}{4}$ cup warm water
3 whole eggs
3$\frac{1}{2}$ cups all-purpose flour
1 egg yolk, lightly beaten
1 teaspoon water

1. In saucepan melt butter. Add cream, sugar, salt, and cardamom. Mix well and cool to lukewarm.
2. In large bowl of mixer sprinkle yeast on warm water; stir to dissolve and let stand for 5 minutes.
3. Add butter mixture, eggs, and 2 cups of the flour to yeast. Mix well, then beat 2 minutes at medium speed.
4. Stir in remaining 1$\frac{1}{2}$ cups flour with a wooden spoon to make a stiff dough. Turn out on lightly floured board and knead until smooth, about 10 minutes.
5. Place dough in greased bowl; turn over to grease top. Cover with a towel and let rise in a warm place, free from draft, until double in bulk, about 1$\frac{1}{2}$ hours.
6. Turn dough out on lightly floured board; knead lightly. Divide the dough into thirds; divide each third in half, then each half into 10 small balls, all the same size. Place three balls in each greased muffin cup.
7. Mix lightly beaten egg yolk with the tablespoon water and brush the tops. Cover and let rise until double in bulk, 30 to 45 minutes.
8. Bake at 375° for 12 to 15 minutes or until golden brown. Serve hot.

   NOTE: Wrap leftover rolls and freeze. When ready to use, sprinkle with water, cover with foil, and reheat at 350.°

Proper storage of bread in the freezer can maintain flavor, freshness, original moisture, and aroma. Wrap freshly baked bread loosely in foil wrap. (If freezing a loaf, cut it in half and wrap each half separately.) Place in moisture-vapor proof container and freeze. To use: heat, uncovered, in a hot oven for about 5 minutes and serve immediately.

WHOLE WHEAT REFRIGERATOR ROLLS

Makes: 30-36 rolls
Temperature: 400°
Baking time: 12-15 minutes
Muffin tins

These are delicious, light rolls that require no kneading!

$\frac{1}{2}$ cup (1 stick butter)
$\frac{1}{3}$ cup shortening
2 cups boiling water
$\frac{1}{2}$ cup packed brown sugar
$1\frac{1}{2}$ teaspoons salt
$\frac{1}{4}$ cup warm water
1 teaspoon sugar
2 packages (2 tablespoons) dry yeast
2 eggs, beaten
$3\frac{1}{2}$ cups whole wheat flour
$2\frac{1}{2}$ cups unbleached all-purpose white flour

1. Melt butter and shortening in boiling water.
2. Add brown sugar and salt; cool.
3. In a small bowl, place the warm water and the sugar; add the 2 packages dry yeast, and stir.
4. Add beaten eggs to cooled butter mixture; add yeast.
5. Mix together whole wheat and unbleached white flour and stir slowly into liquid, a little at a time, just until mixed. Do not knead.
6. Cover tightly with foil and refrigerate for at least 5 hours or overnight.
7. Remove dough from refrigerator 3 to $3\frac{1}{2}$ hours before serving; shape as desired and place in muffin tins.
8. Cover with waxed paper and a light cloth and let rise in a warm place until doubled in size, about 2 to 3 hours.
9. Bake in a preheated oven at 400° for 12 to 15 minutes, or until brown.
10. If desired, brush tops of hot rolls with melted butter.

CORN MEAL REFRIGERATOR ROLLS

Makes: 36 rolls
Temperature: 400°
Baking time: 12-18 minutes
Shallow baking pans

These rolls freeze well. When ready to use, moisten frozen rolls lightly and bake at 300° until heated through.

1¹/₂ cups milk
¹/₂ cup shortening
¹/₂ cup sugar
2 teaspoons salt
2 packages (2 tablespoons) dry yeast
¹/₂ cup warm water (110°-115°)
5 to 5¹/₂ cups unsifted all-purpose flour
2 eggs
1 cup corn meal
¹/₄ cup melted butter

1. Scald milk; stir in shortening, sugar, and salt. Cool to lukewarm in large bowl of electric mixer.

2. Sprinkle yeast on warm water; stir until dissolved.

3. Add dissolved yeast, 2¹/₂ cups of the flour, and eggs to milk mixture. Beat with electric mixer at medium speed for 5 minutes.

4. With wooden spoon, stir in corn meal and enough additional flour to make a soft dough.

5. Turn out on lightly floured board or canvas; knead until smooth, satiny, and no longer sticky, 5 to 8 minutes.

6. Round dough into a ball; place in greased bowl and brush lightly with melted shortening. Cover and let rise in a warm place until double in size, 1 to 1¹/₂ hours.

7. Punch dough down and brush with melted shortening. Cover with waxed paper (or plastic wrap) and a damp cloth. Refrigerate overnight (or as long as 3 days).

8. Remove dough from refrigerator and punch down. Shape into 1¹/₂ inch balls. Dip each in melted butter and place in greased baking pans, about ¹/₄ inch apart. Cover and let rise until nearly double in size, about 45 minutes.

9. Bake in preheated 400° oven 15 to 20 minutes.

SAUCY ORANGE ROLLS

Serves: 20
Temperature: 350°
Baking time: 20 minutes
13 x 9 inch pan

ROLLS
1 envelope (1 tablespoon) dry yeast
1/4 cup warm water
1/4 cup sugar
1 teaspoon salt
2 large eggs
1/2 cup sour cream
6 tablespoons (3/4 stick) butter, melted
3 1/2 cups sifted all-purpose flour

ORANGE FILLING
2 tablespoons melted butter, divided
1/2 cup sugar
2 tablespoons grated orange peel

ORANGE GLAZE
3/4 cup sugar
1/2 cup sour cream
2 tablespoons orange juice
1/2 cup butter

1. Dissolve yeast in warm water in large mixing bowl. Beat in sugar, salt, eggs, sour cream, and melted butter with electric mixter. Gradually add 2 cups of flour. Beat until smooth. Knead remaining flour into dough.

2. Place dough in greased bowl. Cover with plastic wrap and let rise in a warm place until double in bulk, about 2 hours. Punch down and knead dough on well-floured surface about 15 times. Divide dough in half.

3. Roll out half of the dough into a 12 inch circle. Brush with one tablespoon of the melted butter. Sprinkle with half the sugar and orange peel mixture. Cut dough circle into 10 wedges. Roll up each wedge starting at the wide end.

4. Place rolls, pointed ends underneath, in rows in greased 13 x 9 inch pan. Do not crowd. Cover and let rise in warm place until double in bulk, about 1 hour.

5. Bake at 350° for 20 minutes or until golden brown. Top immediately with orange glaze.

ORANGE GLAZE: Combine sugar, sour cream, orange juice, and butter in small sauce pan. Boil for 4 minutes, stirring constantly. Pour over hot rolls. Serve warm. These can be reheated.

JALAPEÑO CORNBREAD

Serves: 20
Temperature: 425°
Baking time: 25 minutes
2 9 x 13 inch baking dishes

2½ cups yellow cornmeal
1 cup flour
1 tablespoon sugar
1 tablespoon salt
4 teaspoons baking powder
3 eggs, lightly beaten
1½ cups milk
½ cup salad oil
1 can (16 ounces) cream-style corn
1 can (4 ounces) diced green chilies
1 can (4 ounces) seeded, chopped
   jalapeño peppers
2 cups grated sharp Cheddar cheese
1 large onion, coarsely grated

1. In large bowl, stir together cornmeal, flour, sugar, salt, and baking powder.
2. In a separate bowl, combine lightly beaten eggs with milk and oil. Add to cornmeal mixture.
3. Stir in corn, green chilies, jalapeño peppers, cheese, and onions.
4. Pour into 2 well-oiled 9 x 13 inch baking dishes.
5. Bake 25 minutes at 425° or until golden brown.

Dry bread crumbs which can be prepared with crusts and crumbs are ingredients in many recipes. Use food processor to pulverize dry bread. Place crumbs in storage jars with tight lids. Freeze. In the freezer, they will keep well for several months.

SPECIAL BISCUITS

Makes: 20 biscuits
Temperature: 400°
Baking time: 30 minutes
9 inch round baking pan

These biscuits are just as good when reheated.

1/2 cup sugar
1/2 cup finely chopped walnuts
3/4 teaspoon cinnamon
1 3/4 cups all-purpose flour
3 teaspoons baking powder
1 teaspoon salt
1/4 cup shortening
3/4 cup (3 ounces) shredded sharp
   Cheddar cheese
1 small apple, peeled, cored and chopped
   (3/4 cup)
2/3 cup milk
1/3 cup butter, melted

1. In a small bowl, stir together sugar, nuts, and cinnamon. Set aside.
2. Into a larger bowl, sift together flour, baking powder, and salt.
3. Cut in shortening. Mix in shredded cheese and apple.
4. Add milk and blend until moistened. This will be a very stiff, almost crumbly mixture.
5. Form into a ball. Flatten dough on floured surface.
6. Divide dough into 20 pieces; shape each into a ball.
7. Roll each ball in melted butter and then in sugar-nutmeat mixture.
8. Arrange in a greased 9 inch round baking pan.
9. Bake at 400° for 30 minutes. Serve hot.

APPLE SPICE MUFFINS

Makes: 12
Temperature: 400°
Baking time: 20 minutes
Muffin tins

2$\frac{1}{4}$ cups flour
$\frac{1}{2}$ cup sugar
3 teaspoons baking powder
1 teaspoon cinnamon
$\frac{1}{4}$ teaspoon cloves
2 beaten eggs
$\frac{1}{3}$ cup oil
$\frac{3}{4}$ cup milk
1 cup diced or grated peeled apples
1 tablespoon grated lemon peel
$\frac{1}{4}$ cup chopped pecans

TOPPING
1 tablespoons butter
2 tablespoons flour
$\frac{1}{4}$ cup packed brown sugar
$\frac{1}{4}$ teaspoon cinnamon

1. Blend together flour, sugar, baking powder, cinnamon, and cloves.

2. Carefully stir in, just enough to moisten, mixture of beaten eggs, oil, and milk.

3. Fold in apples, lemon peel, and pecans.

4. For topping, combine butter, the 2 tablespoons flour, brown sugar, and the $\frac{1}{4}$ teaspoon cinnamon.

5. Spoon batter into 12 greased muffin tins and sprinkle with topping.

6. Bake at 400° for 20 minutes.

BLUEBERRY MUFFINS

Serves: 16-18
Temperature: 375°
Baking time: 25 minutes
2 inch muffin tins

This came from an old hand-written recipe collection.

1¹/₂ cups fresh or frozen blueberries
2¹/₃ cups flour
1 cup sugar
2 teaspoons cream of tartar
1 teaspoon baking soda
¹/₄ teaspoon salt
6 tablespoons butter, room temperature
³/₄ cup milk
1 egg, lightly beaten
¹/₂ teaspoon vanilla

1. Wash and drain the blueberries. Toss the berries with ¹/₃ cup of the flour and set aside.

2. Sift the 2 cups of flour with the sugar, cream of tartar, soda, and salt into a bowl. Cut in the butter with a pastry blender or two knives until the mixture looks like coarse meal.

3. In another bowl combine milk, lightly beaten egg, and vanilla. Add all at once to dry ingredients, stirring just enough to moisten. Fold in blueberry-flour mixture. Do not overmix.

4. Spoon batter into greased 2 inch muffin cups, filling them two-thirds full.

5. Bake in preheated 375° oven for 25 minutes or until golden brown. Serve hot with butter.

HEALTH MUFFINS

Temperature: 400°
Baking time: 18-20 minutes
Muffin tins

You can serve fresh muffins every morning with this mixture in your refrigerator.

2 cups boiling water
2 cups 100% bran cereal or unprocessed bran
(no added sugar)
4 extra large eggs, beaten
1 quart buttermilk
2 cups honey
1 cup salad oil
5 teaspoons baking soda
5 cups whole wheat flour
1 cup wheat germ (not sweetened)
1 teaspoon salt
3 cups 40% bran flakes
2 cups raisins, dates, nuts, or seeds (optional)

1. Pour boiling water over 100% bran; cool.

2. In a large bowl, beat eggs, buttermilk, honey, and oil.

3. Add soda to bran mixture and combine with the liquids.

4. Stir in flour, wheat germ, and salt.

5. Fold in bran flakes and raisins (if desired).

6. Do not stir again.

7. Cover and store in refrigerator up to 6 weeks, using as needed.

8. Spoon into greased muffin tins.

9. Bake in 400° oven for 18 to 20 minutes.

*ORANGE MARMALADE MUFFINS

Makes: 12 muffins
Temperature: 375°
Baking time: 20 minutes

¼ cup shortening
2 tablespoons sugar
1 egg
1½ cups all-purpose sifted flour
½ teaspoon salt
2 teaspoons baking powder
¼ cup milk
2 tablespoons orange juice
1 teaspoon grated orange peel
¾ cup orange marmalade

1. Cream shortening and sugar together.
2. Add egg and beat until fluffy.
3. Sift together the flour, salt, and baking powder.
4. Mix milk, orange juice, orange peel, and marmalade together.
5. Add dry ingredients to creamed mixture alternately with liquids. Mix lightly just until moistened.
6. Spoon batter into 12 greased muffin cups and bake 20 minutes at 375.°

*POPPY SEED MUFFINS

Makes: 2 dozen 1¹/₂ inch muffins
Temperature: 375°
Baking time: 30 minutes

This is a very sweet muffin and cake-like in texture.

> **3 eggs**
> **²/₃ cup oil**
> **1¹/₄ cups evaporated milk**
> **1 teaspoon vanilla**
> **2¹/₄ cups sifted all-purpose flour**
> **1¹/₂ cups sugar***
> **³/₄ cup poppy seeds**
> **4¹/₂ teaspoons baking powder**

1. Mix and beat well the eggs, oil, milk, and vanilla.
2. Sift together the flour, sugar, and baking powder into a bowl. Stir in the poppy seeds.
3. Add the dry ingredients to the liquid ingredients, stirring just enough to moisten.
4. Spoon batter into greased muffin pans, filling two-thirds full.
5. Bake at 375° for 20 minutes, or until golden brown. Serve warm.

   *NOTE: The sugar can be decreased to 1¹/₈ cups without changing the texture, if you prefer a less sweet muffin.

APRICOT
TEA BREAD

Temperature: 350°
Baking time: 50 minutes
8¹/₂ x 4¹/₂ x 2¹/₂-inch pan

¹/₂ cup dried apricots
Cold water to cover
1 large orange
¹/₂ cup seedless raisins
2 cups all-purpose flour
1 teaspoon baking soda
2 teaspoons baking powder
1 cup sugar
¹/₄ teaspoon salt
¹/₂ cup chopped nut meats
1 egg
2 tablespoons melted butter
1 teaspoon vanilla

1. Cover apricots with cold water and let stand ¹/₂ hour. Drain.

2. Squeeze juice from orange; reserve peel.

3. Add enough boiling water to juice to make 1 cup.

4. Put orange peel, apricots, raisins, and nuts through medium blade of food grinder, or chop in processor.

5. Sift flour, soda, baking powder, sugar, and salt into bowl.

6. Add fruit mixture, nut meats, and orange juice.

7. Stir in beaten egg, melted butter, and vanilla.

8. Bake in greased 8¹/₂ x 4¹/₂ inch loaf pan at 350° for 50 minutes.

9. Let stand 10-15 minutes before removing from pan; cool on rack. Serve hot or cold. Very good "freezer and keeper."

BANANA NUT BREAD

Makes: 1 loaf
Temperature: 300°
Baking time: 1 hour
5 x 9 inch loaf pan

Serve with a date or raisin filling as a tea sandwich.

1³/₄ cups sifted flour
¹/₂ teaspoon salt
¹/₂ teaspoon baking soda
1 teaspoon baking powder
2 eggs
¹/₃ cup softened butter
²/₃ cup sugar
2 ripe bananas, cut up
1 cup chopped walnuts

1. Sift flour, salt, baking soda, and baking powder together and set aside.

2. Put the eggs, softened butter, sugar, and bananas in a blender and blend well.

3. Add the blended mixture to the dry ingredients and mix just until moistened; do not beat.

4. Stir in chopped walnuts. Turn into greased loaf pan.

5. Bake in 300° oven for 1 hour. Let stand 10-15 minutes before turning out.

CRANBERRY NUT BREAD

Serves: 12
Temperature: 325°
Baking time: 1 hour
9¹/₂ x 5¹/₂ x 2³/₄ inch loaf pan

2 cups all-purpose flour
¹/₂ teaspoon salt
1¹/₂ teaspoons baking powder
¹/₂ teaspoon baking soda
1 cup sugar
Juice and grated peel of 1 medium orange
2 tablespoons salad oil
Boiling water
1 egg, beaten
1 cup chopped raw cranberries
1 cup chopped walnuts

1. Sift together into bowl the flour, salt, baking powder, baking soda, and sugar.

2. Add orange juice and grated peel. Mix well.

3. To salad oil, add boiling water to measure ³/₄ cup. Stir into above mixture.

4. Add beaten egg and mix well.

5. Stir in cranberries and nuts.

6. Pour mixture into well-greased loaf pan.

7. Bake at 325° for 1 hour or until done.

8. Cool on rack 15 minutes. Remove from pan.

9. Cool thoroughly. Wrap in foil or plastic; store 24 hours before serving.

FRUIT
CROCK JAM

This is a wonderful homemade jam treat that may be replenished throughout the summer with the fruits in season. By the end of summer your jam crock could be a real pot-pourri of fruits. You can make up to 4 cups of jam at one time.

1 cup cleaned fresh fruit*
1 cup sugar

1. Use a deep saucepan and bring the fruit and sugar to a rolling boil.
2. Reduce heat to simmer and cook for 30 minutes, stirring occasionally.
3. Remove from heat and stir constantly for 5 minutes—this is very important.
4. Let cool and pour into crock or very large jar with a lid. Refrigerate. This keeps well.
5. After each addition of cooked fresh fruit or berries, stir well.

   NOTE: It is important to make no more than 4 cups of jam at one time or it will not jell.

   *You may use strawberries, olalliberries, raspberries, cherries, blueberries, blackberries, black raspberries, plums, apricots, etc. It's up to you.

©Steve Crouch

Soups

The season of the year and the entrée determine the soups chosen for Steinbeck House luncheons. The recipes here range from light soups like the Tomato Bouillon, especially welcome on warm September days, to rich ones like the popular Creamy Lettuce Soup or the Artichoke and Chicken Soup, to the hearty ones like the Western Clam Chowder and the Minestrone with Pesto Sauce.

COLD
CRANBERRY SOUP

Serves: 8
3 quart saucepan

A beautiful color, and a delicious stand-up first course.

2 oranges
1 tablespoon butter
1¼ cups sugar
1 cup dry sherry
⅔ cup orange juice
4 cups fresh or frozen cranberries
1 cup dry white table wine
1 cup sour cream
1 cup light cream
1 cup Club soda

1. Remove yellow peel from oranges with a potato peeler, then cut peel in very thin Julienne. Squeeze juice from oranges to make ⅔ cup.

2. In saucepan, melt butter but do not brown. Add orange peel and sauté, stirring until soft. Add sugar, sherry, and orange juice. Heat to boiling; boil for 2 minutes. Add cranberries and cover. Boil for 2 minutes. Uncover and boil for another 3 minutes. Chill. (This can be done a day ahead and chilled overnight.)

3. Place half of chilled mixture in blender, add white wine and blend at moderate speed for 1 minute. Pour into large bowl.

4. Place other half of cranberry mixture in blender, add light cream and sour cream and blend at moderate speed for 1 minute.

5. Combine both mixtures, strain to remove orange rind, cranberry skins and seeds. Just before serving, whisk in Club soda until well blended.

Garnish each serving with a sprig of mint.

GAZPACHO

Serves: 16-20, 1 cup servings

This can be used as either a soup or a salad. It is refreshing for a summer meal and is only 85 calories per serving.

1 clove garlic, cut in half
3 large ripe tomatoes
1 firm cucumber
$^1/_2$ sweet onion
1 medium-size green pepper, seeded
   and chopped
$1^1/_2$ cups sliced fresh mushrooms (12 small)
1 small can (7 ounces) green chili salsa
1 large can (1 quart 14 ounces) tomato juice
2 tablespoons salad oil
2 tablespoons red wine vinegar
2 teaspoons salt
1 teaspoon crushed, dried oregano leaves
1 teaspoon crushed cumin seeds
$^1/_2$ teaspoon coarse black pepper
1 medium-size ripe avocado, cubed,
   for garnish

1. Select a bowl or tureen that will fit in the refrigerator. Rub inside with cut garlic.

2. Dice and combine unpeeled tomatoes and cucumbers. Add chopped onion, sliced mushrooms and chopped green pepper.

3. Add salsa, juice, oil, vinegar, and seasonings.

4. Refrigerate and allow to ripen at least 3 hours. Overnight is better.

5. Serve very cold, topped with cubed avocado as garnish.

*CREAMY
LETTUCE SOUP

Serves: 6

2 tablespoons butter
$\frac{1}{2}$ medium-size onion, chopped
2 tablespoons flour
$\frac{1}{2}$ teaspoon salt
$\frac{1}{8}$ teaspoon pepper
2 beef bouillon cubes
2 cups boiling water
2 cups light cream
$\frac{1}{2}$ teaspoon beef concentrate
2 cups shredded iceberg lettuce
Grated nutmeg or chopped parsley

1. Heat butter in a 2 quart pan and sauté onion until soft.

2. Stir in flour, salt, and pepper and blend until bubbling.

3. Dissolve the bouillon cubes in the boiling water and gradually stir into onion mixture.

4. Add the light cream and the beef concentrate. Reheat slowly to just below boiling point.

5. Divide shredded lettuce into 6 soup bowls.

6. Pour soup mixture over lettuce and serve immediately. Top each serving with grated nutmeg or chopped parsley.

Remember the rule of soup serving: If it is to be a hot soup, serve it steaming hot, and if it is to be a cold soup, have it come to the table icy cold.

*CREAM OF
BROCCOLI LEEK SOUP

Serves: 8

3 tablespoons butter
$1/3$ cup chopped leeks, white only
$1/3$ cup chopped onions
$1/3$ cup sliced celery
1 cup chopped uncooked broccoli
3 tablespoons flour
$1/2$ cup dry white wine
3 cups chicken stock
1 cup light cream
Salt, pepper, and fine herbs or thyme

1. Melt butter in saucepan and sauté leeks, onions, celery, and broccoli for 5 minutes.
2. Blend in flour.
3. Stir in wine and chicken stock, bring to boil, then let simmer until vegetables are tender. Season with salt, pepper, and fine herbs or thyme.
4. Add light cream and heat to serve.

*ZUCCHINI BISQUE

Serves: 6 (6 cups)

Subtle seasoning makes this a beautiful soup.

1 tablespoon butter
1 cup chopped onions
$1^1/2$ pounds shredded zucchini
$2^1/2$ cups chicken broth
$1/8$ teaspoon nutmeg
1 teaspoon dried basil
1 teaspoon salt
1 cup light cream

1. Melt butter and sauté onions until limp.
2. Add zucchini, chicken broth, nutmeg, basil, and salt to onions and simmer, covered, 15 minutes. Cool.
3. Blend zucchini mixture in blender until smooth.
4. Return to saucepan, add cream, and heat to serve.

GABILAN SOUP

Serves: 6

**3 medium-size carrots, cut into 1 inch
matchsticks**
3 celery stalks, cut into 1 inch matchsticks
1½ cups chicken stock
3 tablespoons butter
2 tablespoons onion, finely chopped
¼ cup flour
3 cups chicken stock
1 cup grated sharp Cheddar cheese
**1 small can (8¾ ounces) tomatoes,
undrained, chopped**
12 drops hot pepper sauce
⅛ teaspoon nutmeg
¼ cup dry white wine
1½ cups light cream, heated
Chopped parsley for garnish

1. Add carrots and celery to the 1½ cups chicken stock in a medium-size saucepan. Cook until tender crisp. Set aside.

2. Melt butter in a large saucepan. Add onion and sauté until transparent but not brown.

3. Add flour and blend well. Slowly stir in the 3 cups chicken stock and cook over medium heat, stirring constantly, until mixture thickens.

4. Blend in cheese and stir until cheese melts. Add previously cooked carrots and celery, then add tomatoes, hot pepper sauce, nutmeg, and wine.

5. Just before serving, stir in hot light cream.

6. Garnish with chopped parsley.

*ARTICHOKE AND CHICKEN SOUP

Serves: 4-5

This delicate soup can be served either hot or cold.

> 1 tablespoon butter
> 2 tablespoons oil
> 1 medium onion, finely chopped
> 1 garlic clove, finely chopped or put through
>   garlic press
> 2 cups cooked and diced artichoke bottoms
> 1 scant tablespoon curry powder
> 2½ tablespoons flour
> 2 cups clear chicken broth
> 1 cup light cream
> ¾ cup finely shredded cooked chicken
> Salt and pepper to taste

1. In a saucepan sauté onion and garlic in butter and oil for about 3 minutes or until onion is softened.

2. Add the artichoke bottoms, salt and pepper to taste, and the curry powder.

3. Continue cooking very slowly until mixture is warmed.

4. Stir in flour and add chicken broth gradually, stirring constantly until soup boils.

5. Remove from heat and put through blender.

6. Return to saucepan. Add the light cream and shredded chicken. Taste for seasoning. Reheat and serve.

Toasted bread cubes are an interesting garnish on cream soup. Arrange soft bread cubes on a cookie sheet. Place cookie sheet under a preheated broiler (400°F) or in a slow oven (300°F) and toast until bread cubes are golden brown on all sides, turning occasionally. Sprinkle with garlic or onion salt the last few minutes.

CREAMY CARROT SOUP

Serves: 6

4 cups grated carrots (about 1 pound)
1 large potato, peeled, grated
1 medium onion, grated
2 tablespoons butter
2 cups chicken broth
$\frac{1}{2}$ cup milk
$\frac{1}{4}$ cup well-washed rice
$\frac{1}{8}$ teaspoon nutmeg
$\frac{1}{2}$ teaspoon salt or to taste
1 teaspoon lemon juice
2 to 3 tablespoons whipping cream
Chopped parsley or chives

1. Melt butter in saucepan. Add carrots, potato, onion, and sauté gently for 5 minutes.
2. Add broth, milk, rice, nutmeg, and salt. Bring to a boil, lower heat and cover pan. Simmer gently for 45 minutes to 1 hour.
3. Stir in lemon juice and cream.
4. Purée mixture in blender in two or more batches.
5. Serve immediately or reheat without boiling. Garnish with chopped parsley or chives.

Bread, cut into thin strips, brushed with melted butter, and toasted in the oven is delicious with soup.

CARROT GINGER SOUP

Serves: 8-10

$^3/_4$ cup onion, minced
$^1/_4$ cup peeled and minced ginger root
$^1/_4$ cup clarified butter
6 cups homemade chicken stock
$1^1/_2$ pounds carrots
1 teaspoon sugar
$1^1/_2$ cups light cream
3 tablespoons butter
$^1/_4$ cup all-purpose flour
$^1/_4$ teaspoon cinnamon
1 raw carrot, cut in julienne strips

1. In a saucepan, cook onion and ginger root in clarified butter, over moderate heat, stirring until onion is softened.

2. Add the stock, carrots, and sugar; bring to a boil and simmer the mixture, covered, until the carrots are tender, 15 to 20 minutes.

3. In a blender, or in a food processor fitted with the steel blade, purée the mixture in batches.

4. Stir in light cream and heat the mixture over low heat, stirring occasionally, until hot.

5. In a large saucepan, melt butter over moderate heat; add the flour and cook the roux, stirring, for 4 minutes, or until it is foamy.

6. Stir the carrot mixture into the roux, add the cinnamon and salt and pepper to taste, then simmer for 5 minutes.

7. Pour soup into a heated tureen and garnish with julienned carrot.

CIOPPINO

Serves: 6-8
Large soup pot

You'll need bibs for everyone and lots of paper napkins as this is messy, but good.

$\frac{1}{2}$ cup salad oil
1 large onion, chopped
$\frac{1}{2}$ cup chopped celery
$\frac{1}{2}$ cup chopped green pepper
1 to 2 cloves garlic, pressed
1 large can (28 ounces) whole tomatoes,
   cut up, not drained
1 can (8 ounces) tomato sauce
1 cup water
1 teaspoon dried basil
$\frac{1}{4}$ cup chopped parsley
1 small bay leaf
6 peppercorns
$1\frac{1}{2}$ teaspoons salt
$\frac{1}{4}$ teaspoon pepper
$1\frac{1}{2}$ teaspoons Italian seasoning
$\frac{1}{4}$ pound mushrooms, sliced
1 tablespoon butter
2 bottles (8 ounces each) clam juice
1 cup dry white table wine
1 to $1\frac{1}{2}$ teaspoons beef concentrate
   seasoning
1 pound rock cod or halibut, cut in chunks
2 Dungeness crabs, cleaned and cracked
1 pound prawns
2 pounds clams in shells, scrubbed

1. In salad oil, sauté onion, celery, green pepper, and garlic for 3 to 4 minutes.

2. Add tomatoes, tomato sauce, water, basil, parsley, bay leaf, peppercorns, salt, pepper, and Italian seasoning and simmer, partially covered, for 2 hours. (This stage can be done early in the day.)

3. Sauté mushrooms in butter and set aside.

4. To tomato sauce add clam juice, wine, and beef concentrate; simmer 10 minutes.

5. Add sautéed mushrooms and arrange in layers the cod or halibut, then the crab, shrimp, and clams.

6. Cook, covered, until clam shells open, about 5 minutes.

7. To serve, dish up into deep soup bowls so that each person gets some of each type of seafood as well as the good sauce. Serve with lots of sour dough garlic bread for dunking.

*MINESTRONE WITH PESTO SAUCE

Serves: 10-12

1 tablespoon olive oil
4 slices salt pork, finely diced
1 or 2 cloves garlic, minced
2 cups coarsely chopped onion
3 cans (15 ounces each) pinto beans, undrained
2 cans (10$\frac{1}{2}$ ounces each) beef broth
4 cups water
1 small can (8 ounces) tomato sauce
2 teaspoons salt
1 teaspoon pepper
1 cup zucchini chunks
1 cup sliced celery
1 cup sliced carrots
1 cup chopped cabbage (Savoy)
1 cup green beans (cut-frozen)
1 cup grated potatoes
$\frac{1}{4}$ cup chopped parsley
1 cup broken spaghetti

1. In a large kettle heat oil. Add salt pork and sauté until lightly browned.
2. Stir in onions and garlic and sauté until onions are golden.
3. Purée the pinto beans in blender or processor and add to kettle.
4. Add beef broth, water, tomato sauce, salt, and pepper. Bring to a boil. Taste for seasoning.
5. Add zucchini, celery, carrots, cabbage, green beans, and potatoes. Simmer for 1$\frac{1}{2}$ hours.
6. About 20 minutes before serving, add parsley and spaghetti, stirring occasionally so pasta won't stick to the bottom.
7. Top each serving with a spoonful of pesto sauce.

PESTO SAUCE FOR MINESTRONE
$\frac{1}{4}$ cup ($\frac{1}{2}$ stick) butter, softened
$\frac{1}{4}$ cup grated Parmesan cheese
$\frac{1}{2}$ cup finely chopped parsley
1 clove garlic, crushed
1 teaspoon dry basil leaves
$\frac{1}{2}$ teaspoon dry marjoram leaves
$\frac{1}{4}$ cup olive oil
$\frac{1}{4}$ cup chopped pine nuts or walnuts

1. Blend butter, Parmesan cheese, garlic, basil, and marjoram.
2. Gradually add olive oil and blend together thoroughly.
3. Stir in chopped nuts.

RUSSIAN
CABBAGE BORSCHT

Serves: 5-6

1½ cups thin-sliced, peeled potatoes
1 cup thin-sliced, peeled beets
4 cups chicken broth (or water)
2 tablespoons butter
1½ cups chopped onion
1 teaspoon caraway seeds
2 teaspoons salt
1 large carrot, sliced
1 rib celery, chopped
3 cups chopped cabbage
⅛ teaspoon black pepper
4 teaspoons cider vinegar
4 teaspoons honey
1 cup tomato puree
¼ teaspoon dill weed
Sour cream
Chopped tomato (optional)

1. Cook potatoes, beets, and broth or water in covered saucepan until tender. Do not overcook. Drain but save the liquid.

2. In large kettle, begin cooking onions in the butter. Add caraway seeds and salt and cook until onion is translucent.

3. Add carrot, celery, cabbage, and stock from beets and potatoes. Cook, covered, until vegetables are tender.

4. Add potatoes and beets; season with pepper, vinegar, honey, and tomato puree.

5. Cover and simmer slowly for at least 20 minutes.

6. Top each serving with dill weed, sour cream, and/or chopped tomatoes.

WESTERN CLAM CHOWDER

Serves: 6-8

An honest soup.

>   2 cans (10½ ounces each) whole small
>   clams
>   8 slices bacon, cut into small pieces
>   4 large celery stalks, thinly sliced
>   1 bunch green onions, chopped
>   1 can (1 pound, 13 ounces) solid-packed
>   tomatoes
>   1 tablespoon Worcestershire
>   2 cups water, divided
>   1 bay leaf
>   1 or 2 diced peeled potatoes
>   1 can (8 ounces) tomato sauce

1. Drain and reserve juice from clams.

2. Sauté bacon, celery, and green onion. Add juice from clams and simmer.

3. Chop tomatoes and add.

4. Add Worcestershire, 1 cup of the water, and the bay leaf. Simmer 2½ to 3 hours.

5. Add clams, potatoes, tomato sauce, and remaining 1 cup water. Simmer 15 minutes, or until potatoes are cooked.

6. Thicken or dilute to taste, and serve hot.

Crackers can be pepped up by brushing them lightly with melted butter, then sprinkling with grated cheese, poppy seeds, onion or garlic salt. Place on a cookie sheet and heat in 350° oven for 10 minutes.

*TACO SOUP

Serves: 8

5 cups beef broth
3 cups sliced onions
2 teaspoons Worcestershire
1 teaspoon cumin
$\frac{1}{2}$ teaspoon chili powder
$\frac{1}{4}$ teaspoon cilantro
$\frac{1}{2}$ cup broken tortilla chips
8 slices of tomato
1 cup shredded Cheddar cheese

1. Combine beef broth, onions, Worcestershire, cumin, chili powder, and cilantro and simmer for at least 30 minutes.

2. In bottom of 8 soup bowls place 1 tablespoon broken tortilla chips, 1 slice of tomato, and 2 tablespoons shredded Cheddar cheese.

3. Fill bowls with hot soup and serve immediately.

TORTILLA SOUP

Serves: 4

3 corn tortillas, cut in $\frac{1}{4}$ inch strips
Salad oil
4 cups homemade chicken broth
1 medium sized tomato, peeled, halved, seeded, and chopped
4 green onions, chopped, including part of the tops
Grated Parmesan cheese

1. Sauté tortilla strips until crisp in hot salad oil.

2. Drain strips on paper towels.

3. Bring to boil the chicken broth with the chopped tomato, onions, and tortilla strips.

4. Simmer slowly 15 to 20 minutes.

5. Pour into serving bowls and top with grated Parmesan cheese.

*TOMATO BOUILLON

Serves: 8

$\frac{1}{4}$ cup ($\frac{1}{2}$ stick) butter
2 cups chopped onions
3 cans (16 ounces each) tomatoes
1 quart beef bouillon or broth
1 teaspoon salt
1 teaspoon dill weed
1 tablespoon dried parsley
Dash of pepper
Parmesan cheese to taste

1. In Dutch oven, melt butter; add onions, and sauté until very tender but not brown.
2. Add tomatoes, beef bouillon, salt, dill weed, dried parsley, and pepper. Heat to simmering and cook about 15 minutes.
3. Cool soup, then put through the blender, half or a third at a time.
4. Reheat when ready to serve.
5. Sprinkle Parmesan cheese on each serving.

CHICKEN STOCK

Makes: 3 pints

We are including this because homemade stock improves the flavor of our recipes.

2 quarts water
2 pounds chicken necks, backs, wings
2 medium carrots, trimmed and cut in
　　3 inch pieces
1 stalk celery, cut in 3 inch pieces
2 or 3 celery tops with leaves
1 medium-size onion, quartered
Bouquet garni (1 large sprig of parsley,
　　$\frac{1}{4}$ teaspoon thyme, 3 or 4 peppercorns,
　　1 bay leaf) tied in cheesecloth bag

1. Combine all of the ingredients in a large kettle and heat to boiling; reduce heat and simmer. Skim surface as needed.
2. Cook covered for 3 hours.
3. Strain, then chill the stock. Remove any fat layer.
4. Stock will keep 2 days in the refrigerator or up to 3 months in the freezer.

©Steve Crouch

Salads and Salad Dressings

Salads at Steinbeck House are creative combinations made from the fresh produce of the Salinas Valley--sometimes called the Salad Bowl of the nation. A number of the salad recipes include their own salad dressings; others recommend a dressing especially suited to the salad. Several unusual salad dressings appear separately also.

These cucumber molds are very similar, but we decided to include them both. The Cucumber Almond Mold recipe may be doubled or tripled easily. It has fewer calories than the Cucumber Salad Ring and the almonds add a delightful crunch. The Cucumber Salad Ring is a bit richer and has a delicate tang. Both are very refreshing.

CUCUMBER ALMOND MOLD

Serves: 6-8
1 quart mold

1 package (3 ounces) lime-flavored gelatin
¾ cup boiling water
1 cup cottage cheese
½ cup buttermilk
½ cup mayonnaise
1 teaspoon prepared horseradish
1 teaspoon prepared mustard
1 tablespoon white vinegar
¼ teaspoon salt
Dash white pepper
¾ to 1 cup shredded, unpeeled English
   cucumber, drained and well-packed
⅓ cup toasted slivered almonds

1. Dissolve lime-flavored gelatin in boiling water in medium-sized bowl.
2. Combine cottage cheese, buttermilk, mayonnaise, horseradish, mustard, vinegar, salt, and pepper in blender and blend well.
3. Stir cheese mixture into warm gelatin and chill slightly.
4. Stir in cucumber and nuts and pour into a 1-quart mold.
5. Chill at least 4 hours.

CUCUMBER SALAD RING

Serves: 6
3 cup mold

This would make a nice luncheon entree, if served with fresh bay shrimp.

> 1 package (3 ounces) lime-flavored gelatin
> ³/₄ cup boiling water
> 1 large package (8 ounces) cream cheese
> 1 cup mayonnaise
> 1 teaspoon prepared horseradish
> ¹/₄ teaspoon salt
> 2 tablespoons lemon juice
> ³/₄ cup drained, shredded unpared
>   cucumber
> ¹/₄ cup finely sliced green onion

1. Dissolve gelatin in boiling water.
2. Combine softened cream cheese, mayonnaise, horseradish, salt, and lemon juice, and beat with electric beater until smooth.
3. Add dissolved gelatin; continue beating until well mixed.
4. Chill until partially set.
5. Stir in cucumber and green onions; spoon into a 3 cup mold.
6. Chill at least 4 hours.

Raw cauliflower for a salad: combine 1 cup each of finely chopped raw cauliflower, celery, carrots, and toasted walnuts with 1 cup mayonnaise. Taste and add more salt and lemon juice to suit. Pack into custard cups and chill. Turn out on lettuce and garnish with parsley and cherry tomatoes.

BROCCOLI MOLD

Serves: 12
1¹/₂-quart ring mold

A colorful addition to a plate.

1 large bunch broccoli
1 envelope unflavored gelatin
¹/₄ cup cold water
1¹/₄ cups white veal or chicken stock
3 tablespoons Worcestershire
2 tablespoons lemon juice
¹/₂ teaspoon salt
¹/₄ teaspoon each pepper and hot
   pepper sauce
4 hard-cooked eggs, chopped
³/₄ cup mayonnaise
2 cups cherry tomatoes

1. Wash and trim broccoli; cut into small flowerets.

2. Cook all the broccoli in boiling water until tender; drain.

3. Reserve 6 flowerets and mince the remaining broccoli by hand. There should be 2 cups.

4. In a small bowl, sprinkle gelatin over cold water to soften.

5. In a saucepan, bring the white veal or chicken stock to a boil, add the gelatin, and stir the mixture until the gelatin is dissolved.

6. Remove the stock from heat and add the broccoli, Worcestershire, lemon juice, salt, pepper, hot pepper sauce, and chopped eggs.

7. Stand over ice until it is cool, stirring occasionally, then fold in mayonnaise.

8. Pour into a 1¹/₂-quart ring mold; cover with wax paper; refrigerate until set.

9. Turn onto a serving platter over red leaf or green leaf lettuce; garnish with the reserved flowerets. Pile cherry tomatoes in the center of ring.

BETH'S FRESH SPINACH MOLD

1 package (3 ounces) lemon-flavored gelatin
1 cup boiling water
½ cup mayonnaise
3 tablespoons tarragon vinegar
5 tablespoons water
Pepper
1 cup cottage cheese
1 cup snipped raw spinach
½ cup finely chopped green onions
½ cup finely chopped celery

1. Dissolve gelatin in hot water.

2. Add ½ cup mayonnaise plus the tarragon vinegar and enough cold water to make 1 cup.

3. Add pepper to taste.

4. Mix with rotary beater until smooth; refrigerate until slightly jelled.

5. Add cottage cheese, spinach, celery, and onions. Mix well.

6. Pour into mold or molds and refrigerate until firm.

MOLDED
CRAB SALAD

Serves: 8
2-quart ring mold

3¹/₃ cups tomato juice
1 large package (6 ounces) lemon-flavored
gelatin
Juice of 1 lemon (3 tablespoons)
¹/₄ cup cider vinegar
2 teaspoons salt
¹/₄ teaspoon ground cloves
¹/₂ teaspoon paprika
6 green onions, chopped
1 cup sliced celery
2 cans (6 ounces) crab meat or 2 cups
fresh Dungeness crab
1 jar (5 ounces) stuffed olives,
coarsely chopped

1. Heat 1 cup of the tomato juice to boiling, stir in lemon-flavored gelatin, until dissolved. Add lemon juice, vinegar, salt, cloves, and paprika.

2. Add remaining 2¹/₃ cups (cold) tomato juice. Chill.

3. When gelatin begins to set, add onions, celery, crab, and olives.

4. Pour into oiled 2 quart ring mold and chill overnight.

   NOTE: Canned or fresh shrimp may be used in place of crab, or a combination of both may be used.

For seafood sauce, mayonnaise is the usual; so add your own touch: grated lemon peel, tarragon, finely minced chives or green onion tops are a few possibilities.

CALCUTTA CHICKEN SALAD

Serves: 10-12

This is a hearty main dish salad that needs only the addition of a hot bread to round out the meal.

1 cup shredded coconut
1 cup dark raisins, steamed
1 cup chopped, unsalted peanuts
1 cup diced, barely ripe banana
1 cup diced, unpeeled red apple
1 cup diced, juice-packed pineapple
   (canned is too sweet)*
1 cup sliced celery
2 cups shredded, cooked chicken
1 cup chutney
1 cup mayonnaise
2 tablespoons curry powder
Garnishes (use any or all): cantaloupe,
   candied ginger, fresh grapes, toasted
   coconut slices, fresh lime

1. Stir together all ingredients, except garnishes, very gently, smoothing out top. Cover with plastic wrap and refrigerate overnight.

2. Serve on lettuce-lined plate, or on circles of peeled cantaloupe with lettuce leaves. Garnish as desired.

   *NOTE: Do not use fresh pineapple as it will tenderize the chicken too much and change consistency of salad.

RICE SALAD
WITH SHRIMP

Serves: 10-12

This salad is a nice accompaniment to barbecued meat or picnic food. The mixture also may be used to stuff 10-12 medium-size tomatoes, peeled and hollowed out, served as a salad on a bed of lettuce.

2 cups long-grain white rice
$\frac{1}{4}$ cup vegetable oil
$\frac{1}{3}$ cup white vinegar
$\frac{1}{2}$ teaspoon salt
$\frac{1}{4}$ teaspoon pepper
$\frac{1}{4}$ teaspoon dried tarragon
$\frac{1}{2}$ green pepper, seeded and minced fine
$\frac{1}{2}$ cup minced fresh parsley
$\frac{1}{2}$ cup minced green onions (include tops)
1 cup cooked green peas
$\frac{1}{2}$ to 1 pound cooked and cleaned
baby shrimp
$\frac{1}{2}$ cup sliced ripe olives
Watercress for garnish

1. Cook rice according to package directions.

2. Place hot rice in large bowl. Add oil, vinegar, salt, pepper, and tarragon. Toss lightly to blend well. Cool to room temperature.

3. Add green pepper, parsley, green onions, and peas. Mix well. Cover bowl and refrigerate for at least two hours.

4. Serve on a chilled serving platter, garnished with the shrimp, olives and watercress.

BEAN SPROUT SALAD WITH DILL DRESSING

Serves: 6

DRESSING
3 tablespoons wine vinegar
8 tablespoons olive oil
$\frac{1}{2}$ teaspoon salt
$\frac{1}{2}$ teaspoon black pepper
1 teaspoon soy sauce
1 tablespoon chopped fresh dill
$\frac{1}{4}$ teaspoon dry mustard
Dash of Worcestershire

8 ounces (3 cups) bean sprouts, roots
   removed, blanched
6 ounces (1 cup) baby shrimp
1 cup thinly sliced celery
$\frac{1}{2}$ cup shredded lettuce
6 cherry tomatoes, halved, or $\frac{1}{2}$ red
   bell pepper, thinly sliced

1. Mix vinegar, oil and seasonings thoroughly.
2. Combine sprouts, shrimp, celery, and lettuce. Toss with dressing just before serving. Garnish with cherry tomatoes or strips of red bell pepper.

PETITS POIS SALAD

Makes a distinguished entrée or salad.

> **2 packages (10 ounces each) frozen
>   petit peas**
> **2 cups sliced celery**
> **¹/₂ cup chopped green onions**
> **¹/₂ cup chopped cashew nuts**
> **¹/₂ cup crumbled fried bacon**
> **1¹/₄ cups Herb Dressing (see below)**

1. Thaw the frozen peas (do not cook). Combine with celery, green onions, cashews, and crisp bacon.
2. Toss with Herb Dressing (see below).
3. Serve on a bed of lettuce surrounded by tomato wedges

or

Use mixture to fill a large tomato, almost cut through in quarters, with "petals" turned back, when set on a lettuce leaf.

> **HERB DRESSING**
> **1 cup sour cream**
> **1 cup real mayonnaise**
> **1 egg-sized onion, chopped**
> **1 clove garlic, minced or mashed**
> **2 tablespoons lemon juice**
> **1 teaspoon chopped parsley**
> **¹/₂ teaspoon salt**
> **¹/₈ teaspoon ground pepper**
> **¹/₄ teaspoon paprika**
> **¹/₈ teaspoon curry powder**
> **¹/₄ teaspoon each dried rosemary
>   and thyme**
> **1 teaspoon caraway seeds**
> **¹/₂ teaspoon Worcestershire**

1. Combine sour cream and mayonnaise. Season with onion, garlic, lemon juice, parsley, salt, pepper, paprika, curry, dried herbs, caraway seeds, and Worcestershire.
2. Chill for 24 hours.

CURRIED
SPINACH SALAD

Serves: 6-8

This salad dressing has a real "zing."

1 pound bacon, fried crisp
1 hard-cooked egg, chopped
2 bunches spinach (1½ pounds), washed,
   trimmed, and torn into pieces

DRESSING
⅔ cup salad oil
¼ cup white wine vinegar
2 tablespoons dry white table wine
2 teaspoons soy sauce
1 teaspoon each sugar, pepper, dry mustard,
   and curry powder
½ teaspoon salt
½ teaspoon garlic powder

1. Toss crisp bacon and chopped egg with clean, torn spinach.

2. Put oil, vinegar, wine, soy, and seasonings in a jar and shake well.

3. Pour dressing over spinach just before serving, and toss well.

SPINACH AND APPLE SALAD

Serves: 6-8

1 bunch fresh young spinach leaves
5 slices bacon, cooked and crumbled
5 green onions, thinly sliced
½ cup salted sliced almonds
1 red Delicious apple, quartered
   and thinly sliced
½ cup cubed Monterey Jack cheese

DRESSING
¼ cup olive oil
3 tablespoons white wine tarragon vinegar
1 teaspoon sugar
½ teaspoon dry mustard
Seasoned salt and seasoned pepper to taste

1. Wash spinach thoroughly, remove stems, spin dry, and tear into bite-size pieces.

2. Combine spinach, crisp bacon bits, green onions, almonds, apple, and cheese in a bowl.

3. Mix together olive oil, tarragon vinegar, sugar, and dried mustard and pour over the salad ingredients. Toss lightly. Salt and pepper to taste.

The Glorious Grape

A heaping cluster of plump grapes rounds out your fruit bowl. Incidentally, grapes will keep longer if stored unwashed in plastic bags in your refrigerator. Bring them out for the festivities, but don't let them sit around, unrefrigerated, for long stretches of time.

AUTUMN FLOWERET SALAD

This is a fall salad since it can be made only with fresh red pimiento.

> 4 cups fresh cauliflower flowerets, cut small
> 1½ cups chopped fresh pimiento, drain
>   juice, reserve
> ½ cup finely sliced green onions,
>   including tops
> ¼ cup chopped dry white onion
> ¼ cup finely chopped parsley
> ¾ cup mayonnaise
> ¾ cup sour cream
> 1 to 2 teaspoons reserved pimiento juice
> ¾ teaspoon salt
> ¼ teaspoon black pepper

1. Place flowerets in bowl.

2. Add pimiento. (Pimiento may be chopped in food processor with quick on/off power. There will be more juice than if hand chopped.)

3. Add onions and parsley.

4. Mix together mayonnaise, sour cream, juice, salt, and pepper. Stir in. Taste for seasoning.

5. Chill well. Serve in lettuce cups. Garnish with chopped parsley.

Tips on Seeding Grapes

The easiest way to get the seeds out of a grape is to cut it in half and flick out the seeds with the point of your knife. Some grape-seeders recommend cutting grapes crosswise a little above center. Since the seeds are usually together, all you have to do is remove them from the larger half, not both halves.

ORANGE WALNUT SALAD

Serves: 5-6

1 teaspoon butter
1/4 cup coarsely chopped walnuts
1 head Bibb lettuce
1/2 pound spinach, stems removed
2 medium-size oranges, peeled, seeded,
   and sectioned
1 small-size sweet onion cut crosswise,
   thinly sliced and pulled into rings

1. Melt butter in heavy skillet over medium heat. Add nuts and stir until lightly browned. Set aside.

2. Wash, dry, and refrigerate lettuce and spinach until crisp. Tear into bite-size pieces.

3. Mix greens, orange sections, and onion rings in salad bowl. Sprinkle toasted walnuts over top.

4. Add only enough sweet and sour dressing (see below) to coat greens. Toss lightly.

SWEET AND SOUR DRESSING

Makes: 3/4 cup

1/2 teaspoon paprika
1/2 teaspoon celery seeds
1/4 teaspoon salt
1/2 teaspoon grated onion
1/4 cup sugar
1/2 cup salad oil
1/4 cup cider vinegar

1. Combine all ingredients in a jar with a tight-fitting lid. Shake until sugar is dissolved and seasonings are well blended. Chill.

2. Shake well before tossing with salad ingredients.

OLD FASHIONED SLAW – STEINBECK FAMILY

Makes: 2 quarts

1 medium head cabbage
1 small onion
1 large green pepper
18 (approximate) stuffed green olives,
     sliced
1 tablespoon celery seed
²/₃ cup sugar
¹/₂ cup salad oil
¹/₂ cup cider vinegar
1 teaspoon salt
1 teaspoon prepared mustard

1. Shred or chop cabbage, onion, and green pepper.

2. Sprinkle sliced olives and celery seed over vegetables.

3. In a small saucepan, combine and bring to a boil sugar, oil, vinegar, salt, and mustard.

4. Add hot liquid to vegetables.

5. Mix well, cover, and let stand for 24 hours before serving.

COLORFUL CARROT SALAD

Serves: 8-10

5 cups diagonally sliced fresh carrots
1 green pepper, sliced lengthwise, seeded,
   and cut into thin strips
1 red onion, peeled and sliced in thin rings
1 can (10 ounces) pitted ripe olives,
   drained
1 can (10 ounces) tomato soup
1/2 cup salad oil
2 tablespoons sugar
1/2 cup red wine vinegar
1 teaspoon Dijon mustard
1 teaspoon celery salt
1 tablespoon Worcestershire
1/4 teaspoon black pepper
1/4 teaspoon liquid hot pepper
1/2 teaspoon garlic powder or 2 cloves
   garlic, minced or mashed

1. Prepare vegetables.
2. Blanch sliced carrots in boiling water for 6 to 8 minutes. Drain and cool.
3. Mix together in saucepan the tomato soup, salad oil, sugar, vinegar, mustard, salt, Worcestershire, pepper, liquid pepper sauce, and garlic and simmer 5 to 10 minutes. Cool.
4. Toss cooled carrots, green pepper, red onion, and olives with dressing.
5. Refrigerate 3 to 4 hours. Serve with a background of lettuce leaves.

   NOTE: This salad will keep up to 10 days.

82

*MARINATED BROCCOLI

Serves: 8-10 as a side dish

2 bunches broccoli
Pimiento for garnish

1. Wash and cut broccoli into serving-size pieces with about 2 inches of stem.
2. Drop into boiling water, being sure that each piece is covered with water. Cook for 5 to 7 minutes. Drain.
3. Run cold water over broccoli to stop cooking; drain, cover, and chill.
4. When ready to serve, pour marinade (see below) over broccoli which has been arranged on butter lettuce to appear to form a head of un-cut broccoli. (Do not let stand over $1/2$ hour before ready to serve or it will turn brown.)
5. Garnish with pieces of pimiento for color.
6. Serve the mayonnaise sauce (see below) on the side.

MARINADE
$2/3$ cup salad oil
$1/2$ teaspoon grated lemon peel
$2/3$ cup lemon juice
1 teaspoon Dijon mustard
1 teaspoon dried basil
1 teaspoon dried marjoram
$1/4$ teaspoon pepper
$1/2$ teaspoon garlic salt
$1/2$ teaspoon celery salt
2 green onions, chopped

1. Combine all marinade ingredients in a jar.
2. Shake well and refrigerate.

MAYONNAISE SAUCE
$2/3$ cup mayonnaise
$1/3$ cup sour cream
2 teaspoons lemon juice
1 teaspoon sugar
$1/2$ teaspoon celery salt
$3/4$ teaspoon dry mustard
$1^1/2$ teaspoons Dijon mustard
1 hard cooked egg, chopped

1. Mix mayonnaise, sour cream, and lemon juice well.
2. Stir in seasonings and chopped egg. Refrigerate.

*MARINATED ZUCCHINI

Serves: 12

6 young zucchini
¹/₄ teaspoon each: sugar, salt, garlic powder,
    and onion powder
2 tablespoons water
¹/₄ cup white wine vinegar
¹/₄ cup medium sauterne
¹/₂ cup salad oil
2 tablespoons each: finely chopped green
    pepper, finely chopped parsley, and
    finely chopped green onions
3 tablespoons sweet pickle relish
Garnish with egg yolk, cherry tomatoes, etc.

1. Cut off ends of zucchini, and slice diagonally about ¹/₈ inch thick.
2. Combine sugar, salt, garlic powder, and onion powder; stir in water, vinegar, sauterne, and oil; then add the chopped green pepper, parsley, and green onions, and the pickle relish.
3. Pour marinade over zucchini and marinate overnight.
4. Before serving, drain well. Serve on red leaf-lettuce garnish with sieved egg yolk, cherry tomatoes, etc.

MARINATED MUSHROOM SALAD

Serves: 4

You can easily add or subtract these ingredients to serve a twosome or a crowd.

12 small fresh mushrooms
"Favorite Vinaigrette Dressing" (see page 86)
2 avocados
12 cherry tomatoes
Salad greens

1. Marinate whole mushrooms in Favorite Vinaigrette Dressing (see page 86) to cover overnight. Turn about 4 times.
2. Arrange on large lettuce leaf: avocado slices, cherry tomatoes (halved), and marinated mushrooms.
3. Drizzle with the marinade.

ANN'S FRENCH DRESSING

Makes: 1 pint

This recipe comes from the elite Blackstone Hotel of the 1930's in Omaha, Nebraska.

6 tablespoons lemon juice
¹/₂ cup water
¹/₂ cup sugar
¹/₂ cup catsup
1 teaspoon dry mustard
1 teaspoon salt
5 tablespoons cider vinegar
1 teaspoon paprika
1 teaspoon Worcestershire
1 cup salad oil

1. Boil lemon juice, water, and sugar into a thin syrup and cool.

2. In bowl or blender, combine syrup with catsup, mustard, salt, vinegar, paprika, and Worcestershire.

3. Beat mixture, gradually adding oil as mixture thickens. Works well in blender.

FRUIT SALAD DRESSING

Makes: 1 pint

This dressing is equally good on salad greens.

¹/₂ cup small curd cottage cheese
5 tablespoons orange juice
1 teaspoon curry powder
¹/₄ teaspoon powdered ginger
¹/₄ teaspoon cinnamon
¹/₂ cup thinly sliced celery
¹/₂ cup sour cream
¹/₂ cup chopped walnuts

1. Blend cottage cheese, orange juice, curry powder, ginger, and cinnamon in blender until smooth.

2. Stir in sour cream, celery, and walnuts.

FAVORITE VINAIGRETTE DRESSING

Makes: 2¹/₂ cups

This is enough marinade for 1 pound of mushrooms. (See Marinated Mushroom Salad, page 84.)

> **1 whole clove garlic, halved**
> **1 cup white wine vinegar**
> **1¹/₂ cups salad oil**
> **1 tablespoon catsup**
> **1 teaspoon sugar**
> **2 teaspoons Worcestershire**
> **¹/₂ teaspoon salt**
> **¹/₂ teaspoon pepper**
> **¹/₄ teaspoon dried basil**
> **¹/₄ teaspoon dry mustard**
> **1 teaspoon parsley flakes**
> **¹/₈ teaspoon horseradish powder**

1. In a blender, mix all ingredients together well.
2. Refrigerate in a tightly covered jar.

Pimiento-caper dressing is wonderful with most cold vegetables. Try it with thinly sliced flowerets of a fresh, white cauliflower. In a jar, combine 1¹/₂ cups oil, (part olive, if you wish) and ¹/₂ cup wine vinegar with ¹/₄ cup chopped pimiento, ¹/₄ cup capers, 1 clove mashed garlic, 2 teaspoons salt, pepper to taste, ¹/₂ teaspoon dill weed and ¹/₂ teaspoon dried tarragon. Shake well and pour over the cold vegetable. Chill for an hour before serving.

SPICY SALAD DRESSING

Makes: 1 cup

This dressing, used on salad greens, goes well with Mexican dishes.

> 1 teaspoon cumin seed
> 1 teaspoon dry mustard
> 1 teaspoon garlic salt
> 2 teaspoons sugar
> 1/2 teaspoon garlic powder
> 1/4 teaspoon black pepper
> 1 teaspoon Worcestershire
> 1 teaspoon Angostura Bitters
> 1 teaspoon dried oregano
> 3 tablespoons red wine vinegar
> 4 to 8 tablespoons salad oil
> Salad greens
> 1/4 cup Parmesan cheese

1. With mortar and pestle, grind or mash together cumin, mustard, garlic salt, sugar, garlic powder, pepper, Worcestershire, bitters and oregano, adding enough cold water to make a slurry (about 1 tablespoon).

2. Let stand for 5 minutes.

3. Add the wine vinegar and the salad oil. Stir thoroughly.

4. Sprinkle salad greens liberally with Parmesan cheese.

5. Add dressing, toss well, and serve.

ROQUEFORT SALAD DRESSING

Makes: 2¹/₂ cups

Serve this on greens, tomatoes, even spinach, to give your taste buds a treat.

> **2 tablespoons minced onion**
> **1 clove garlic**
> **8 ounces (1 cup) cottage cheese**
> **3 ounces Roquefort cheese**
> **3 to 4 drops hot pepper sauce**
> **1 tablespoon Worcestershire**
> **1 tablespoon steak sauce**
> **2 tablespoons lemon juice**
> **1 cup mayonnaise**
> **³/₄ cup buttermilk**

1. Put ingredients, in order given, in blender or food processor and mix until well blended.
2. Refrigerate in covered container.

HIGHLANDER "MAYONNAISE"

Makes: 1²/₃ cups

Here's a recipe from New Zealand. The unique combination is especially good on fresh fruit.

> **¹/₂ can sweetened condensed milk**
> **¹/₂ cup vinegar or lemon juice**
> **2 egg yolks**
> **¹/₂ teaspoon salt**
> **1 teaspoon dry mustard**
> **Dash of cayenne pepper**

1. Place all ingredients in a blender and whirl until mixture thickens.
2. This salad dressing can be stored in a cool place for 1 week.

SALAD DRESSING FOR LEAF LETTUCE

Makes: 1¹/₃ cups

1 cup salad oil
¹/₃ cup red wine vinegar
1 tablespoon water
1 teaspoon garlic salt
1 teaspoon coarse-ground pepper
1 teaspoon dry mustard
¹/₄ teaspoon sugar
1 teaspoon dried summer savory
Salad greens such as iceberg lettuce, red leaf lettuce, green leaf lettuce, romaine, endive, and escarole.

1. Put oil, vinegar, water, and seasonings in a quart jar.

2. Shake well for 30 seconds.

3. Pour over tender salad greens and toss lightly.

HERB SEASONING

Makes: 5 tablespoons

Beth Ainsworth recommends this in place of salt.

4 tablespoons parsley flakes
1 teaspoon garlic powder (not salt)
2 teaspoons onion powder (not salt)
2 teaspoons paprika
2 teaspoons thyme
2 teaspoons marjoram

1. Combine all ingredients and store in a tightly covered jar. Use as you would salt.

2. Other dried herbs which could be added or substituted, as you wish, are celery flakes, basil leaves, tarragon, oregano, and chervil.

©Steve Crouch

Entrees

Delicious and unusual entrées have been developed by Valley Guild cooks. Among the entrées here are a number that can be prepared in advance and thus free the hostess from last-minute preparations. At Steinbeck House, the luncheon entrée is presented with a side dish or vegetable and a colorful garnish.

CHICKEN SUPREME IN PASTA RING

Serves: 6
Temperature: 350°
Baking time: 45 minutes
9 inch ring mold

PASTA RING
1 cup uncooked elbow macaroni
1½ cups milk
1 cup soft bread crumbs (firmly packed)
¼ cup (4 tablespoons) butter
1 cup grated Cheddar cheese
3 slightly beaten eggs
1 chopped pimiento
2 tablespoons grated green pepper
1 tablespoon instant minced onion
½ teaspoon Worcestershire
½ teaspoon salt
¼ teaspoon pepper

1. Cook macaroni in boiling salted water just until tender; drain well.
2. In saucepan, combine milk, bread crumbs, butter, and grated cheese; stir over very low heat just until cheese is melted.
3. Add macaroni, beaten eggs, pimiento, green pepper, onion, Worcestershire, salt, and pepper.
4. Pour into well-greased 9 inch ring mold, set in shallow pan, pour in 1 inch hot water. Bake in a moderate oven (350°) about 45 minutes, or until firm.
5. Remove mold from water. Let stand on rack 5 minutes before turning out on heated platter. Fill with the following:

Continued...

CHICKEN SUPREME
4 tablespoons butter
$\frac{1}{2}$ cup minced onion (medium size)
3 tablespoons flour
1 cup sour cream
$\frac{3}{4}$ cup chicken stock
$\frac{1}{4}$ cup dry white table wine
1 tablespoon parsley flakes
$\frac{1}{2}$ teaspoon Worcestershire
$\frac{1}{4}$ teaspoon paprika
Salt and pepper to taste
2 cups coarsely diced cooked chicken
(or turkey)
1 small can (4 ounces) sliced mushrooms,
drained

1. Melt butter in top of double boiler over direct heat; add onion and sauté gently for 5 minutes; do not brown.
2. Blend in flour; add sour cream and stock; cook, stirring constantly, until mixture boils and thickens.
3. Place pan over hot water. Add remaining ingredients. Heat thoroughly before serving in center of ring mold.
4. Garnish with strips of pimiento, bunches of parsley, or cherry tomatoes.

    NOTE: Two cups of crabmeat or shrimp can replace the chicken. Or you can substitute two 7 ounce cans water-packed tuna. Drain, rinse, and break into large pieces the tuna before adding to the sauce.

SAN FRANCISCO CHICKEN

Serves: 6

> 6 boned and skinned chicken breasts
>   (3 whole breasts cut in half)
> 3 tablespoons flour
> 1/8 to 1/4 teaspoon nutmeg
> 1/4 teaspoon white pepper
> 1/4 cup each margarine and butter
> 1/2 cup chicken broth
> 1/2 cup California Rosé wine
> 1/2 teaspoon grated lemon peel
> 3 tablespoons chopped green onions
> 6 English muffins, split, toasted,
>   and buttered
> 6 thick slices tomato

1. Dredge chicken on both sides in mixture of flour, nutmeg, and pepper.

2. Melt butter and margarine in large Dutch oven; brown chicken on both sides.

3. Add chicken broth, wine, lemon peel, and green onions. Cover and simmer until chicken is tender, about 30 minutes.

> **SOUR CREAM TOPPING**
> 1 cup sour cream
> 2 tablespoons chopped pimiento
> 2 tablespoons chopped parsley
> 1 teaspoon lemon juice
> 1 or 2 drops Tabasco

1. Mix sour cream, pimiento, parsley, lemon juice and Tabasco thoroughly.

TO ASSEMBLE:

2. Place half a toasted and buttered muffin on plate, add slice of tomato; top with a chicken breast.

3. Spoon on a little chicken pan gravy, if desired, and then swirl on a spoonful of the sour cream topping.

4. Serve other half of muffin on the side.

   NOTE: Chicken could be served on cooked broccoli or asparagus spears instead of muffin.

HOT CHICKEN ARTICHOKE BOTTOMS

Serves: 4
Temperature: 350°
Baking time: 20-25 minutes
Shallow casserole

If you wish to make an impression, serve this to your guests.

4 cooked artichoke bottoms
1 whole chicken breast, cooked and cubed

1. Place artichoke bottoms in shallow casserole and top with the cubed chicken. Set aside.

TOMATO-MUSHROOM SAUCE
3 tablespoons butter
$\frac{1}{2}$ pound mushrooms, sliced
1 teaspoon finely chopped shallots
$\frac{1}{3}$ cup dry white table wine
2 tomatoes, peeled, seeded, and coarsely
   chopped
1 cup heavy cream

1. Melt butter in saucepan. Add mushrooms, shallots, and wine and cook until liquid is reduced by half.

2. Add tomatoes and cook briskly until most of the liquid is cooked away.

3. Stir in cream and continue cooking until cream is reduced by half.

WHITE SAUCE
2 tablespoons butter
2 tablespoons flour
$\frac{3}{4}$ cup milk
Salt
Cayenne

1. Melt butter in saucepan; remove from heat and stir in 2 tablespoons flour.

2. Add milk and stir the sauce over medium heat until it comes to a boil.

3. Season to taste with salt and cayenne.

4. Add the white sauce to the tomato-mushroom sauce and blend well.

5. Pour sauce over the chicken-filled artichoke bottoms.

6. Bake at 350° for 20 to 25 minutes.

MUSHROOMS WITH HAM AND ARTICHOKES

Serves: 8
Temperature: 400°
Baking time: 15-20 minutes
9 x 13 inch pan

Serve hot as a main course for luncheon or as a side dish for dinner.

16 large or 24 medium-size mushrooms
3 tablespoons minced green onion, divided
5 tablespoons butter or margarine
1 package (9 ounces) frozen artichoke
  hearts, thawed and chopped
1 cup finely chopped cooked ham
1 teaspoon summer savory leaves, crushed
¼ teaspoon salt
½ cup soft bread crumbs (about one slice
  firm white bread, whirled in blender
  or processor)
1 egg, lightly beaten
3 tablespoons grated Parmesan cheese
¼ cup dry white table wine
Parsley for garnish

1. Wipe mushrooms clean with a damp cloth. Remove stems and chop fine.

2. In frying pan sauté stems and onion in 2 tablespoons of the butter until onion is limp.

3. Remove from heat and stir in chopped artichoke hearts, ham, summer savory, salt, bread crumbs, and egg.

4. Melt remaining 3 tablespoons butter in 9 x 13 inch pan. Turn mushroom caps in butter to coat. Leave in pan, open side up.

5. Fill caps with artichoke mixture, rounding tops and pressing in firmly. Sprinkle tops with Parmesan cheese.

6. Pour wine into pan around mushrooms. Bake, uncovered, 15 to 20 minutes in 400° oven. Garnish with parsley.

ARTICHOKE BAKE

Serves: 4
Temperature: 375°
Baking time: 20 minutes

**12 to 16 small artichokes, about 3 inches
  long, not including stem
Acid water (1 tablespoon vinegar to each
  1 quart water)
Boiling salted water
1 package (3 ounces) cream cheese,
  room temperature
$^1/_4$ cup chopped chives, fresh, frozen, or
  freeze-dried
$^1/_4$ cup ($^1/_2$ stick) butter, room temperature
Salt and pepper
$^1/_2$ cup grated Parmesan cheese**

1. Cut top third from each artichoke, peel off outer leaves down to pale green inner ones, and cut in half lengthwise. Drop in acidified water to prevent darkening.

2. Put artichokes in enough boiling salted water to barely cover; cover pan and cook 10 to 15 minutes, or until artichokes are easily pierced. Drain well.

3. Arrange artichokes close together in a single layer in a buttered shallow baking dish (one from which you can serve).

4. Blend cream cheese with chives and butter.

5. Sprinkle artichokes with salt and pepper, then dot evenly with cream-cheese mixture, and sprinkle evenly with Parmesan cheese. (You can cover and chill dish at this point until ready to heat.)

6. Bake in a moderately hot oven, 375,° for 20 minutes, or until cheese is golden.

Serve a simple butter sauce with artichokes. In a small saucepan, melt one cup butter. Add $^1/_4$ cup lemon juice; $^1/_4$ cup fresh, chopped parsley; 1 teaspoon salt; $^1/_2$ teaspoon dry mustard; and a dash of hot pepper sauce (Tabasco). Cook over low heat 5 minutes. Stir before serving. Serve warm with hot artichokes.

ARTICHOKES IN TOMATO SAUCE

Serves: 6-8

A classic combination of tomato sauce, artichokes, pasta, and cheese.

**12 to 16 small artichokes (about 2 inches
   in diameter or less)
Juice of 1 lemon
$\frac{1}{3}$ cup olive oil
2 cloves garlic, chopped
1 large onion, chopped
1 carrot, peeled and shredded
4 large tomatoes, peeled, seeded,
   and chopped
$\frac{1}{2}$ cup dry white table wine
$\frac{1}{2}$ teaspoon dried thyme, basil, or oregano
Salt and pepper
Hot spaghetti or other pasta
Freshly grated Parmesan cheese**

1. Trim stems, tops, and tough leaves from artichokes and, with scissors, cut tips from remaining leaves.

2. Cover artichokes with water to which lemon juice has been added. Cook at a slow boil until artichokes are easily pierced through the bottom (20 to 30 minutes).

3. Drain and cut in half lengthwise. Remove any fuzzy choke and discard.

4. Heat oil in large heavy saucepan and sauté garlic, onion, and carrot until crisp-tender, about 5 minutes.

5. Stir in tomatoes, wine, and thyme. Simmer 2 to 3 minutes or until bubbly.

6. Add halved artichokes and spoon sauce over them. Season to taste with salt and pepper.

7. Cover and simmer gently 10 to 15 minutes, or until artichokes are tender and tomatoes are saucy.

8. Serve artichokes with the sauce over or surrounded by cooked spaghetti.

9. Sprinkle generously with Parmesan cheese.

ARTICHOKE VERONIQUE

Serves: 6

6 large artichokes
1$\frac{1}{2}$ teaspoons salt
6 tablespoons lemon juice (2 lemons)
$\frac{1}{2}$ cup butter
$\frac{1}{4}$ cup finely chopped onion
$\frac{1}{3}$ cup flour
$\frac{1}{8}$ teaspoon each black pepper, dry mustard,
**   and ground nutmeg**
2$\frac{1}{4}$ cups milk
1 cup heavy cream
1 egg, slightly beaten
4 ounces ($\frac{1}{4}$ pound) Swiss cheese, grated
2 cups diced cooked lobster
$\frac{1}{2}$ cup seedless grapes
$\frac{1}{2}$ cup dry white table wine

1. Remove about 1 inch from tops of artichokes by cutting straight across with a sharp knife. Cut off stems about 1 inch from base. Remove and discard lower outer leaves. With scissors, clip off tips of remaining leaves. Soak artichokes 20 to 30 minutes in cold water and lemon juice. Rinse and drain.

2. Put the artichokes and 1$\frac{1}{2}$ teaspoons of salt into a large saucepan or kettle; add enough boiling water to cover. Bring to boil. Cook 35-45 minutes or until a leaf can be pulled out easily.

3. While artichokes are cooking, heat butter in the top of a double boiler. Add onion and cook over medium heat about 3 minutes. Stir in mixture of flour, salt, pepper, mustard, and nutmeg. Heat until bubbly. Remove from heat and gradually add milk and cream, stirring constantly until smooth. Bring to boil; boil 1 minute, continuing to stir.

4. Mix a small amount of the hot mixture with the egg and stir into hot white sauce. Place sauce over hot water, in bottom of double boiler, and cook over simmering water 3 to 5 minutes, stirring occasionally.

5. Add the cheese and stir until cheese is melted. Stir in lobster, grapes, and wine; heat thoroughly.

6. Spread each artichoke open and pull out center leaves. Using a spoon, remove and discard the "choke" or fuzzy part. Transfer artichokes to a heated platter.

7. Fill the artichokes with the sauce.

99

POPPY'S VEGETABLE POT

Serves: 15-20
Large cooking pot with
tight-fitting lid

This recipe is great to serve at a barbecue. It is interesting because each vegetable retains its own flavor.

Cauliflower leaves
5 medium carrots, cut in 3 inch lengths
3 medium potatoes, scrubbed and cut
in quarters
10 small fresh artichoke hearts, trimmed
(top, bottom, and outside leaves)
1½ pounds fresh broccoli, cut in 4 or
5 inch pieces, using flowers and
peeled stems
1 head of cauliflower (6 to 7 inches in
diameter), cut in quarters
1 medium-size head of cabbage,
cut in quarters
2 medium-size yellow onions, peeled and
cut in quarters
5 cloves of garlic, peeled and left whole
Salt and pepper
¼ cup olive oil
Water

1. Wash all vegetables well.

2. Place leaves of cauliflower on bottom of very large stove-top cooking pot.

3. Layer vegetables in order given: longer cooking vegetables on bottom, shorter cooking vegetables on top.

4. Sprinkle each layer with salt and pepper.

5. Pour olive oil over top and add enough water to cover 1 inch of bottom of the pot.

6. Bring water to a boil, then cover tightly and simmer about 45 minutes, or until vegetables are just tender.

7. Drain liquid and pour vegetables carefully onto a large serving platter.

   NOTE: You could use carrots, broccoli, and cauliflower with onion, garlic, and olive oil to taste. Cook the same way.

*SOLE FLORENTINE

Serves: 6
Temperature: 350°
Baking time: 25-30 minutes
Shallow baking dish

STUFFED FILLETS
6 medium-size sole fillets (about 2 pounds)
2 tablespoons butter
2 tablespoons minced onion
1 package (10 ounces) frozen chopped
   spinach, thawed
2 tablespoons flour
2 tablespoons fine dry bread crumbs
$1/2$ cup shredded Swiss cheese
$1/2$ teaspoon salt
$1/4$ teaspoon hot pepper sauce
1 cup buttered bread crumbs
Mushroom sauce
Parsley sprigs and lemon wedges

1. Wash and dry fillets of sole.
2. To make spinach filling, melt butter in saucepan, stir in onion and spinach. Stir over medium heat until onions are soft, about 5 minutes.
3. Blend in flour and dry bread crumbs. Cook, stirring until mixture simmers. Remove from heat and stir in cheese, salt, and hot pepper sauce.
4. Place $1/4$ to $1/3$ cup spinach filling in center of each fillet. Roll up and place seam side down in buttered shallow baking dish.
5. Spoon mushroom sauce (*see below*) over fish, coating well. Cover with the buttered bread crumbs.
6. Bake at 350° for 25 to 30 minutes, or until fish flakes easily when tested with a fork.
7. Garnish with parsley sprigs and lemon wedges.

MUSHROOM SAUCE
6 tablespoons butter
$3/4$ cup chopped fresh mushrooms
4 tablespoons flour
2 cups milk
$1/8$ teaspoon hot pepper sauce
Salt and pepper to taste

1. Melt 2 tablespoons of the butter in heavy skillet and sauté mushrooms over medium-high heat about 2 minutes. Set aside.
2. Melt the remaining 4 tablespoons butter in sauce pan over medium heat. Blend in flour. Gradually add milk, stirring constantly. Heat and continue to stir until thickened.
3. Add seasonings and sautéed mushrooms.

ASPARAGUS CHEESE ROLLS WITH CRAB FLAMBÉ

Serves: 6
Temperature: 475°
Baking time: 10-15 minutes
Cookie sheet

ASPARAGUS CHEESE ROLLS
24 asparagus spears, small to medium size
1½ cups sifted all-purpose flour
½ teaspoon salt
½ cup shortening
⅓ cup grated Cheddar cheese
3 to 4 tablespoons ice water

1. Wash asparagus well and break off the tough ends. Peel two inches from the lower part of the spears with a swivel-blade peeler.

2. Place asparagus in a large skillet and cover with boiling water. Cover skillet with a tight-fitting lid. Cook over moderate-high heat for 4 or 5 minutes or until barely tender. Drain and plunge into ice water. Place on paper towels to dry and chill.

3. Sift flour and salt into a bowl. Using a pastry blender or two knives, cut in the shortening until mixture forms coarse crumbs. Add cheese and toss to mix.

4. Sprinkle the water over the mixture gradually, stir and press with a fork until mixture begins to hold together. Shape into a ball.

5. Place dough on a lightly floured pastry cloth or board. Roll into a rectangle ⅛ inch thick. Cut into 6 pieces measuring 6 x 4 inches each. Place 4 asparagus spears in the center of each rectangle and roll, then fold over the ends. Place on a cookie sheet. The rolls may be refrigerated at this time for several hours.

6. Bake in a preheated 475° oven for 10 to 15 minutes (5 minutes longer if refrigerated) or until golden brown.

7. Serve with crab flambé.

Continued...

CRAB FLAMBÉ
¼ cup (4 tablespoons) butter
¼ cup flour
1½ cups chicken stock
1 cup chicken bouillon cube
1 cup light cream
2 teaspoons Dijon mustard
Salt and white pepper to taste
2 tablespoons butter
2 cups fresh crab meat
⅓ cup brandy
1 tablespoon dry sherry
4 tablespoons chopped parsley

1. Melt the ¼ cup butter in a saucepan. Add flour and blend over low heat for 2 minutes.
2. Add chicken stock and bouillon cube; stir constantly until sauce starts to thicken.
3. Add the light cream; continue to cook over medium-low heat, stirring until thick.
4. Add mustard, salt and pepper. Keep warm.
5. In skillet melt the 2 tablespoons butter. Add crab meat and toss to coat crab.
6. Heat brandy and sherry in a small pan. Pour over crab and ignite. Toss lightly. Simmer for a few minutes.
7. Combine crab with creamed mixture.
8. To serve, place baked Asparagus Cheese Rolls on a heated platter or individual plates. Pour crab mixture over top and garnish with chopped parsley.

FILLETS OF SOLE QUEEN VICTORIA

Serves: 6

This is a very delicate and quite elegant fish dish.

8 fillets of sole or flounder (2½ pounds)
1 egg white
¾ cup heavy cream
½ teaspoon salt
2 tablespoons chopped parsley
2 drops hot pepper sauce
1 cup dry white table wine
½ cup water
1 small onion, sliced thin
3 slices of lemon
1 bay leaf
3 whole black peppercorns
1 teaspoon salt
¼ teaspoon dried tarragon

1. Rinse fillets under cold water and pat dry with paper towels. Select 6 of the best-looking fillets and set aside.

2. Cut remaining fillets into 1 inch pieces. Place in blender with egg white, cream, salt, parsley, and hot pepper sauce. Blend at high speed 1 minute (less if using a food processor) until mixture is smooth and light green in color.

3. Place the 6 reserved fillets, dark side up, on cutting board. Spoon 2 rounded tablespoons of the fish mixture over each fillet, leaving a ½ inch edge all around. Starting at narrow end, roll fillets and fasten with toothpicks.

4. Lightly butter a medium-sized deep skillet. Place fillets in skillet in an upright position on their broader, more even ends, so that they barely touch the sides of the pan.

5. Add wine, water, onion, lemon slices, bay leaf, peppercorns, salt, and tarragon. Bring liquid to a boil, cover pan, reduce heat to low and simmer 10 minutes, or until centers are just firm when tested with a fork. Do not overcook.

6. Remove fillets from pan with slotted spoon or spatula. Drain well, reserving stock. Place on heated platter and keep warm. Serve with Newburg Sauce.

Continued...

NEWBURG SAUCE
3 tablespoons butter
2 tablespoons flour
$1/4$ teaspoon salt
$1/2$ teaspoon paprika
$3/4$ cup light cream
$1/2$ cup reserved fish stock
2 egg yolks
2 tablespoons dry sherry

1. Melt butter in medium saucepan. Stir in flour, salt, and paprika until blended. Cook, stirring, several minutes.
2. Gradually stir in cream and fish stock. Cook over medium heat, stirring until mixture thickens and boils. Boil 1 minute.
3. Beat egg yolks in bowl. Stir in $1/3$ cup of the hot sauce; then stir egg mixture into the sauce. Add sherry. Stir over low heat just until thick.
4. Spoon some of the sauce over the fish rolls and serve the remainder in a separate bowl. Garnish the platter with parsley and lemon wedges.

MYSTERIOUS STRIPED BASS

Elaine Steinbeck

I'm not sure who invented this recipe. I think it just growed. John and I used to visit Nathaniel and Marjorie Benchley in Nantucket, and they would pay us back by coming to see us in Sag Harbor. Whenever—we would fish together and cook the catch.

This simple broiled striped bass takes on mystery because nobody can figure out the delicate subtle flavor. It comes from just plain old gin. Maybe one night when we were cooking, the gin bottle was handy.

The dried minced onion gives a crunch and the gin gives a punch.

Behead, skin and fillet fish. If time allows, sprinkle with lemon juice and refrigerate. Preheat broiler to high. Place fish in a shallow buttered pan. Sprinkle with salt and pepper, melted butter, lemon juice, and dried minced onions. Put under broiler and cook until lightly brown. Then add more melted butter if needed and two to four ounces of gin, depending on the size of the fillets. Put back under broiler to flambé and cook until brown.

CRAB AND ASPARAGUS CASSEROLE

Serves: 6
Temperature: 350°
Baking time: 20 minutes
8 x 8 x 2 inch casserole

3 tablespoons butter
3 tablespoons flour
1¹/₂ cups milk
1 teaspoon salt
¹/₈ teaspoon pepper
¹/₂ teaspoon Worcestershire
¹/₂ cup grated sharp Cheddar cheese
¹/₂ teaspoon dry mustard
4 hard-cooked eggs
2 cups fresh crab meat, or 2 cans
  (7 ounces each) crab meat
1 pound fresh asparagus, cooked

1. Melt butter in saucepan. Stir in flour and mix until bubbly.

2. Stirring constantly, gradually add milk; cook until smooth and thick.

3. Add salt, pepper, Worcestershire, ¹/₄ cup of the cheese, and dry mustard. Stir until cheese melts; remove from heat.

4. Peel and quarter 3 of the eggs. Reserve 1 egg to slice for garnish.

5. Combine sauce with eggs and crab meat.

6. In small 8 inch square buttered baking dish, arrange asparagus spears so points will show.

7. Pour crab sauce over asparagus. Sprinkle with remaining ¹/₄ cup of cheese.

8. Bake for 20 minutes 350° preheated oven.

9. Garnish with remaining egg.

   NOTE: 1 pound fresh broccoli, cut into spears and cooked, may be substituted for asparagus.

*SHRIMP CREOLE

Serves: 8

The sauce for this dish must be prepared a day in advance.

$1/4$ cup ($1/2$ stick) butter, melted
1 green pepper, chopped
$1/2$ pound fresh mushrooms, sliced
1 cup finely chopped onion
3 tablespoons flour
1 teaspoon chili powder
1 teaspoon salt
$1/4$ teaspoon pepper
1 clove garlic, minced
1 bay leaf
$1/2$ teaspoon celery seeds
$1/4$ teaspoon powdered thyme
2 cups tomato juice
2 cups chopped, peeled tomatoes
1 pound cleaned, medium-size, uncooked
   shrimp
1 tablespoon minced parsley
6 cups rice (cooked in chicken broth)

1. Melt butter in skillet and saute, over low heat, the green pepper, mushrooms, and onion for 15 to 20 minutes.
2. Blend in flour, chili powder, salt, pepper, garlic, bay leaf, celery seeds, and thyme.
3. Gradually add tomato juice and tomatoes and simmer for 2 minutes.
4. Refrigerate overnight.
5. When ready to serve, add shrimp and parsley to hot sauce and simmer for 20 minutes.
6. Serve creole with rice cooked in chicken broth.

SHRIMP CURRY

Serves: 6-8

3 tablespoons butter
¼ cup thin-sliced onions
½ cup sliced carrots
½ cup thin-sliced green beans
1 to 2 tablespoons curry powder
3 tablespoons flour
2½ cups canned or chopped fresh tomatoes
1 bottle (8 ounces) clam juice
½ cup chopped, peeled tart apple
1 tablespoon chutney
3 pounds cleaned and cooked medium-size
    shrimp

1. Melt butter; add onions, carrots, and green beans; and cook over low heat until onion is transparent.

2. Stir in curry powder and cook a few seconds longer.

3. Add flour and mix well.

4. Stir in tomatoes, clam juice, apple, and chutney; simmer for 5 minutes.

5. Add shrimp and simmer for 5 minutes. If sauce is too thick, add more clam juice.

6. Serve with steamed rice and an assortment of condiments such as coconut, chutney, chopped hard-cooked eggs, chopped peanuts, chopped banana, crumbled bacon, diced tomatoes, chopped scallions, raisins, and pineapple bits.

The greatest sin in cooking any shellfish is to overcook. Prawns react by getting tough and shrinking so you actually get less meat for your money. Length of time of simmer-cooking will vary according to size, but 5 minutes should be long enough for the biggest prawn.

SEAFOOD IN CHEESE SAUCE

Serves: 5
Temperature: 350°
Baking time: 25-30 minutes
1 quart casserole or individual
shells

3 tablespoons butter
3 tablespoons flour
1⅓ cups light cream
½ teaspoon salt
2 tablespoons butter
2 ounces (¾ cup) mushrooms, sliced
2 tablespoons chopped celery
2 teaspoons chopped green pepper
2 tablespoons chopped green onions
3 tablespoons chopped black olives
1½ teaspoons chopped pimiento
⅓ pound (1 cup) shrimp
⅓ pound (1 cup) crab
1⅓ cups grated sharp Cheddar cheese
Freshly ground pepper to taste

1. Melt the 3 tablespoons butter in a saucepan. Stir in flour until well blended.

2. Add light cream slowly, stirring constantly until mixture boils and thickens. Add salt. Set aside.

3. Melt the 2 tablespoons butter in a medium-size skillet. Sauté sliced mushrooms, green pepper, and green onions, stirring 2 or 3 minutes. Remove from heat. Add ripe olives and pimiento.

4. Combine white sauce, vegetable mixture, shrimp, crab, and 1 cup of the grated cheese. Cook over low heat just until cheese melts. Season to taste.

5. Pour into buttered shallow casserole; sprinkle with the remaining ⅓ cup grated cheese.

6. Bake, uncovered, at 350° for 25 to 30 minutes or until bubbly. Serve with rice.

SHRIMP WITH PASTA

Serves: 5-6
Temperature: 325°
Baking time: 50 minutes
9 x 13 inch baking dish

12 ounces mostaccioli (medium-size pasta)
8 ounces mozzarella cheese, grated
$\frac{1}{4}$ cup grated Romano cheese
$\frac{1}{4}$ cup grated Parmesan cheese
$\frac{1}{2}$ cup (1 stick) butter
$\frac{3}{4}$ cup white table wine
3 to 4 cloves garlic, finely chopped
1$\frac{1}{2}$ teaspoons chopped onion
1$\frac{1}{2}$ teaspoons lemon juice
1 pound medium-size shrimp, cleaned
   and cooked
1 cup chopped parsley
$\frac{1}{4}$ pound mushrooms, sliced
Paprika

1. Boil pasta according to package directions. Rinse and drain and place in 9 x 13 inch baking dish or casserole.

2. Mix $\frac{1}{2}$ of all grated cheeses into cooked pasta and set aside.

3. In large skillet, melt butter and add wine, garlic, onion, and lemon juice. Bring to a simmer, then add shrimp and $\frac{1}{2}$ cup of the parsley. Bring back to a simmer and add mushrooms.

4. Using all the liquid, stir shrimp mixture into pasta in baking dish.

5. Add the other half of Romano and Parmesan cheeses and mix.

6. Top with remaining mozzarella cheese and the other $\frac{1}{2}$ cup chopped parsley. Sprinkle with paprika.

7. Cover and bake at 325° for 35 minutes. Uncover and finish baking for 15 minutes.

A pasta such as macaroni and spaghetti, will almost double in bulk when cooked; egg noodles will stay the same; while one cup of uncooked rice will equal three cups when cooked.

110

*ASPARAGUS AND HAM TIMBALES

Serves: 6-8
Temperature: 350°
Baking time: 35-40 minutes
6 to 8 ³/₄ cup ovenproof molds

2 pounds asparagus, tough ends removed
1 cup light cream
³/₄ cup fresh bread crumbs, well packed
¹/₂ cup minced onion
2 tablespoons butter
³/₄ cup chopped baked ham
¹/₃ cup freshly grated Parmesan cheese
¹/₃ cup grated Swiss cheese
5 large eggs, beaten
Salt and freshly ground pepper
Pinch of nutmeg
2 cups Hollandaise sauce (see below)
Garnish — paprika

1. Cut asparagus in ¹/₃ inch pieces. Blanch in boiling water until tender-crisp. Drain well in colander.
2. Preheat oven to 350.° Generously butter timbale cups.
3. Combine light cream with bread crumbs and set aside.
4. Sauté onions in melted butter until soft but not browned. Add ham and heat through.
5. Combine cheeses, beaten eggs, and bread crumb mixture. Stir in drained asparagus and seasonings. Spoon into molds.
6. Place molds in a pan with 1 inch of boiling water. Bake 35 to 40 minutes or until a toothpick inserted in center comes out clean.
7. Remove molds from water-bath and let stand 5 minutes.
8. Unmold on hot serving platter. Serve with Hollandaise sauce and garnish with paprika.

HOLLANDAISE SAUCE
6 egg yolks
¹/₄ cup lemon juice
1 cup (2 sticks) butter, melted
¹/₄ cup hot water
¹/₄ teaspoon salt
Cayenne pepper to taste

1. Whisk egg yolks until smooth in top of double boiler over hot (not simmering) water.
2. Beat in lemon juice. Gradually add very hot melted butter, whisking constantly.
3. Whisk in hot water and add seasonings to taste. Continue beating 1 minute or until well blended.

TRIPLE CHEESE SOUFFLÉ

Serves: 6 (as first or main course)
Temperature: 375°
Baking time: 40-50 minutes
6 cup soufflé dish or 6 individual baking dishes

Most soufflés depend on a thick white sauce to hold everything together. Not this beauty! Cream cheese does the job and also gives the cook a lot of leeway. Blend it ahead and leave at room temperature for a couple of hours before baking. Even refrigerate, but bring to room temperature before baking. You can freeze, too; bake an extra 50 minutes. And prepare for compliments.

> **6 eggs**
> **¹/₂ cup heavy cream**
> **¹/₄ cup grated Parmesan cheese**
> **¹/₂ teaspoon dry mustard**
> **¹/₂ teaspoon salt**
> **¹/₄ teaspoon white pepper**
> **¹/₂ pound medium-sharp Cheddar cheese**
> **11 ounces cream cheese, softened**
> **1 tablespoon butter**

1. In a 6-8 cup blender, place the eggs, cream, Parmesan cheese, mustard, salt, and pepper. Blend until smooth.

2. With blender running, break off pieces of Cheddar cheese and add to the mixture. Then drop in chunks of cream cheese. After all the cheese is incorporated, blend the mixture at high speed for 5 seconds.

3. Grease a 6 cup soufflé dish with the butter. Pour in the cheese mixture and place in preheated 375° oven.

4. If the soufflé is to be served as a first or main course, bake for 40-45 minutes. (For individual soufflés, bake 15-20 minutes.) The top should be nicely browned and, when dish is shaken, the center should jiggle just a bit. If it is to be served as a hot cheese course, or if you prefer a firm soufflé, bake until the mixture is completely set and the surface is cracked (about 45 to 50 minutes).

5. Serve at once while still hot. If the dish must be held, turn off oven and open the door a crack so that the soufflé will not overbake.

*HAM AND CHEESE SOUFFLÉ

Serves: 6-8
Temperature: 375°
Baking time: 40-45 minutes
2 quart souffle dish

2 tablespoons grated Parmesan cheese
¹/₄ cup (¹/₂ stick) butter
1¹/₂ cups milk
3¹/₂ tablespoons tapioca
¹/₂ teaspoon salt
1 teaspoon Dijon mustard
¹/₈ teaspoon cayenne pepper
1 cup shredded sharp Cheddar cheese
6 egg yolks, well beaten
1 cup ground cooked ham
6 egg whites

1. Butter well a 2 quart soufflé dish and sprinkle the bottom and sides with the grated Parmesan cheese. Shake off excess cheese, reserving it. Refrigerate dish so cheese will cling.

2. Melt the butter in a heavy saucepan. Add the milk; heat until warm. Stir in tapioca and let stand 5 to 10 minutes.

3. Over medium heat, bring milk to a full boil, stirring constantly. Remove from heat and add salt, mustard, cayenne pepper, grated Cheddar cheese, and any excess Parmesan from coating the dish.

4. Stirring well with a wire whip, add the well beaten yolks to the base. Blend in the ground cooked ham.

5. Beat the egg whites until stiff but not dry. Using whisk, vigorously stir about ¹/₄ of the whites into the base.

6. Pour the base over the remaining beaten whites and carefully fold together. Turn the mixture into the prepared chilled dish and smooth the top with a spatula. Run your thumb around the mixture near the rim. (This will give the baked souffle a "hat.")

7. Bake in 375° oven 40 to 45 minutes, or until set and golden. Serve at once.

SPINACH CUSTARD

Serves: 6
Temperature: 350°
Baking time: 45 minutes
6 x 9 x 1½ inch baking dish

1½ pounds fresh spinach, trimmed
1 small onion, minced
1 clove garlic, minced
1 tablespoon olive oil
2 large eggs
¾ cup light cream
¼ teaspoon grated nutmeg
⅛ teaspoon salt
¼ teaspoon dried basil
⅛ teaspoon pepper
⅔ cup day-old bread crumbs
⅓ cup freshly grated Parmesan cheese
2 tablespoons chopped parsley

1. Wash the spinach well and cook in a covered saucepan, in the water that clings to the leaves, until wilted, about 2 to 3 minutes. Drain thoroughly and chop. (There should be ¾ cup).

2. In a small skillet, sauté onions and garlic in olive oil until soft but not brown. Cool.

3. In a bowl, whisk eggs until frothy. Add light cream, nutmeg, salt, basil, and pepper. Add chopped spinach, onion, bread crumbs, Parmesan cheese, and parsley. Mix well.

4. Spread mixture in a buttered 6 x 9 x 1½ inch pan. Bake at 350° for 45 minutes or until firm and lightly browned.

5. To serve, cut into squares and garnish with additional parsley sprigs.

QUICHE CRUST

Makes: 2 10 inch crusts

3 cups all-purpose flour
1 teaspoon salt
¼ cup butter
1 cup shortening
1 egg, slightly beaten
1 tablespoon vinegar
¼ cup water

1. Mix together flour, salt, butter, and shortening until it forms pea-sized lumps.
2. Add beaten egg, vinegar, and water and mix all together until it forms a ball. Divide in half.
3. Roll out one of the halves on lightly floured board until large enough circle to fit into 10-inch quiche or pie pan. Press on bottom and sides of pan and flute edges.

*HAM LEEK QUICHE

Serves: 7
Temperature: 350°
Baking time: 45 minutes
9 inch pie pan

1 partially baked 9 inch quiche crust
5 leeks
¼ cup (½ stick) butter
4 eggs
1 cup light cream
½ cup heavy cream
½ teaspoon salt
¼ teaspoon pepper
⅛ teaspoon nutmeg
½ cup grated Swiss cheese
⅔ cup chopped ham

1. Clean leeks, cut off the green leaves and discard, using only the white part. Cut this into thin strips and chop.
2. Sauté chopped leeks in butter.
3. In mixer bowl, combine eggs, light cream, heavy cream, salt, pepper, and nutmeg and beat until well blended.
4. In the bottom of partially baked crust, sprinkle Swiss cheese, ham, and sautéed leeks. Pour cream mixture over all.
5. Bake in 350° oven for about 45 minutes, or until set.

*SPINACH RICOTTA QUICHE

Serves: 7
Temperature: 350°
Baking time: 45 minutes
10 inch pie pan

1 partially cooked quiche crust
¼ pound bulk pork sausage
⅓ cup chopped onion
2 cups light cream
4 eggs
½ teaspoon salt
½ teaspoon dried basil leaves
¼ teaspoon pepper
1 container (8 ounces) ricotta cheese
1 package (10 ounces) frozen chopped
spinach, thawed and squeezed dry
1 cup grated mozzarella cheese

1. Cook sausage, crumble, and drain off excess fat.

2. Add the chopped onion and cook until onion is limp.

3. Heat the light cream. Cool.

4. In a large mixing bowl, beat the eggs, salt, basil leaves, and pepper. Beat in ricotta cheese and light cream.

5. Spread the spinach, mozzarella cheese, and cooked sausage evenly in the bottom of partially cooked quiche crust; pour egg and milk mixture over top.

6. Bake at 350° for about 45 minutes or until set. Let stand a few minutes before serving.

BROCCOLI CHEESE PIE

Serves: 6-8
Temperature: 400° 15 minutes
375° 20-25
minutes
10 inch pie pan

A handsome custard in a tender cheese crust.

CHEESE CRUST
1 cup grated Cheddar cheese
³/₄ cup flour
¹/₂ teaspoon salt
¹/₄ teaspoon dry mustard
¹/₄ cup (¹/₂ stick) melted butter

1. Using pastry blender, combine cheese with flour, seasonings, and melted butter.
2. Press on bottom and sides of 10-inch pie pan.

FILLING
2 cups chopped, cooked fresh broccoli
1 tablespoon butter
1 medium onion, chopped
¹/₄ pound sliced fresh mushrooms
2 tablespoons flour
1 cup light cream
1 teaspoon salt
¹/₄ teaspoon nutmeg
Dash of pepper
3 eggs, slightly beaten

1. In a saucepan, sauté onions and mushrooms in butter. Stir in the 2 tablespoons flour; add light cream, salt, nutmeg, and pepper. Simmer 1 minute.
2. Add broccoli and beaten eggs. Blend well.
3. Pour into 10 inch unbaked cheese crust.
4. Bake at 400° for 15 minutes. Reduce heat to 375° and bake 20 to 25 minutes or until knife inserted in center of pie comes out clean.

QUICHE LORRAINE

Temperature: 425° 10 minutes
325° 25 minutes
10 inch pie or quiche dish

1 pound bacon, fried and crumbled
1 unbaked 10 inch pastry shell
1 cup ($^1/_4$ pound) grated Swiss cheese
4 eggs
2 cups light cream
$^1/_4$ teaspoon each salt, pepper, and sugar
Dash each nutmeg and cayenne

1. While bacon is frying, pre-bake pastry shell at 425° for 10 minutes or until very lightly browned. Remove from oven.

2. Sprinkle crumbled bacon and then grated cheese evenly over pie crust.

3. Beat eggs lightly; add cream and seasonings and mix well.

4. Pour mixture over bacon and cheese.

5. Bake at 425° for 10 minutes and then at 325° for 25 minutes or until a knife inserted in filling comes out clean.

Eggs should be removed from the refrigerator thirty minutes before using in order to give a larger volume.

MUSHROOM ARTICHOKE PIE

Serves: 6
Temperature: 350°
Baking time: 25-30 minutes
9 inch pie pan

A mushroom-cracker "crust" sets this apart.

6 petite artichokes
$1/2$ pound fresh mushrooms, coarsely
   chopped
3 tablespoons butter
5 tablespoons crushed salted crackers
$3/4$ cup chopped green onions
1 tablespoon butter
2 cups shredded Monterey Jack cheese
1 cup cottage cheese, small curd
3 eggs
$1/4$ cup light cream
$1/4$ teaspoon cayenne
$1/4$ teaspoon paprika

1. Boil artichokes 6 minutes, or until fork tender. Drain and cool.
2. Sauté chopped mushrooms in the 3 tablespoons butter.
3. Stir crushed crackers into mushrooms. Press into buttered 9 inch pie pan to make the "crust." Chill to harden butter.
4. Sauté green onions in the tablespoon of butter. Spread over mushroom "crust."
5. Coarsely chop artichokes and sprinkle over green onion.
6. Sprinkle with shredded Monterey Jack cheese.
7. Put cottage cheese, eggs, light cream, cayenne, and paprika into a blender and run until smooth.
8. Pour over other ingredients in "crust."
9. Bake at 350° for 25 to 30 minutes or until set in center.
10. Let stand for 10 minutes before cutting in wedges.

*EMPANADA QUICHE

Serves: 8
Temperature: 375°
Baking time: 45 minutes
10 inch pie pan

10 inch prepared quiche shell
$\frac{1}{4}$ pound grated Monterey Jack cheese
$\frac{3}{4}$ pound ground beef
1 tablespoon butter
3 tablespoons green onion, chopped
1 clove garlic, minced
$\frac{1}{2}$ teaspoon salt
$\frac{1}{2}$ teaspoon cumin
$\frac{1}{2}$ teaspoon chili powder
$\frac{1}{8}$ teaspoon pepper
1 medium-size tomato, peeled, halved,
   seeded, and chopped
$\frac{1}{4}$ cup raisins
6 medium-size pimiento-stuffed olives,
   sliced
1 can ($2\frac{1}{2}$ ounces) chopped green chilies
4 eggs, slightly beaten
$1\frac{1}{2}$ cups light cream
$\frac{1}{4}$ teaspoon salt
$\frac{1}{4}$ teaspoon nutmeg

1. Partially bake quiche shell at 350° for 8 minutes. Be sure to prick shell before baking.

2. In bottom of quiche shell, sprinkle the grated Jack cheese.

3. Brown ground beef, drain off excess fat, and set aside.

4. In butter, sauté green onion and garlic with salt, cumin, chili powder, and pepper. Remove from heat.

5. Add meat and stir in tomato, raisins, olives, and green chilies. Spread over grated cheese in crust.

6. Mix together the eggs, light cream, the $\frac{1}{4}$ teaspoon salt, and nutmeg. Pour over meat mixture.

7. Bake at 375° for 45 minutes. Let rest 15 to 20 minutes before serving.

CRÊPES

Makes: 30

     1 cup cold water
     1 cup cold milk
     4 eggs
     $\frac{1}{2}$ teaspoon salt
     2 cups flour, sifted
     $\frac{1}{4}$ cup butter, melted

1. In blender, combine cold water, milk, eggs, salt, and flour and blend on high speed for 1 minute.
2. Add melted butter and blend for 2-3 seconds more.
3. Let set at least 2 hours before cooking.

*CRÊPES CARLOTTA WITH SPICY SAUCE

Serves: 6
Temperature: 350°
Baking time: 25 minutes
8 x 8 x 2 inch pan

FILLING
$1\frac{1}{3}$ cups diced cooked chicken
$2\frac{1}{2}$ tablespoons chopped green chilies
$\frac{1}{3}$ cup chopped green onions
$\frac{1}{3}$ cup chopped ripe olives
1 cup grated sharp Cheddar cheese
1 cup grated Monterey Jack cheese
12 crêpes
Sour cream and green onion garnish

1. Mix chicken with green chilies, green onion, olives, and cheeses.
2. Fill each crêpe with $\frac{1}{4}$ cup of filling. Roll and place in oiled baking pan.
3. Cover and bake at 350° for 25 minutes.
4. Serve 2 per person in ramekins. Top each serving with $\frac{1}{4}$ cup spicy sauce (see below) and garnish with dollop of sour cream and chopped green onion.

SPICY SAUCE
$\frac{1}{3}$ cup enchilada sauce
$\frac{1}{3}$ cup tomato sauce
$\frac{1}{3}$ cup green chili salsa
$\frac{2}{3}$ cup chopped, seeded tomato

1. Mix the three sauces and heat gently for a few minutes.
2. Add chopped tomato and continue heating, just until tomato is warm.
3. Spoon over cooked crêpes.

BROCCOLI AND CHICKEN CRÊPES

Serves: 8
Temperature: 325°
Baking time: 30 minutes
9 x 13 inch pan

3 tablespoons finely-chopped onion
⅓ pound mushrooms, sliced
2 tablespoons butter
2 tablespoons flour
½ cup light cream
¼ cup chicken broth
2 tablespoons grated Parmesan cheese
1 can (4 ounces) water chestnuts, drained
   and chopped
1 teaspoon salt
⅛ teaspoon pepper
1 teaspoon dried marjoram
1 cup chopped cooked chicken (1 chicken
   breast)
2 cups chopped cooked broccoli
16 7 inch crêpes

1. Sauté onion and mushrooms in butter.

2. Stir in the flour, light cream, and chicken broth; cook until thickened.

3. Add the Parmesan cheese, water chestnuts, salt, pepper, and marjoram. Mix well.

4. Mix in the chicken and broccoli; remove from heat.

5. Fill each crêpe with about 1 tablespoon of mixture; roll. Place in 9 x 12 inch pan. Spoon over following sauce.

Continued...

DOUBLE CHEESE SAUCE
$^1/_4$ cup (4 tablespoons) butter
$^1/_4$ cup flour
$^3/_4$ cup light cream
1 cup milk
2 tablespoons grated Parmesan cheese
1 cup grated Swiss cheese, divided
2 teaspoons Dijon mustard
$^1/_4$ teaspoon salt
$^1/_4$ teaspoon nutmeg
$^1/_8$ teaspoon cayenne pepper
3 tablespoons dry white table wine
Paprika

1. Make a roux with the butter and flour.
2. Stir in light cream, milk, Parmesan cheese, $^1/_2$ cup of the Swiss cheese, mustard, salt, nutmeg, cayenne pepper, and wine. Stir until smooth.
3. Pour mixture over rolled crêpes and sprinkle with the other $^1/_2$ cup grated Swiss cheese.
4. Bake at 325° until bubbly, about 30 minutes.
5. Sprinkle with paprika before serving.

Make frittata your Friday special. Sauté diced zucchini, chopped green pepper and onion, minced garlic and parsley in olive oil. Add a chopped tomato (squeeze out seeds and juice) and basil. Pour over seasoned eggs (one per person), cook without stirring for a minute or so. Sprinkle with Parmesan and slide under the broiler to lightly brown the top. Cut in wedges to serve. Artichoke hearts, mushrooms may be added to sauté.

CHICKEN ARTICHOKE CRÊPE

Serves: 8
Temperature: 350°
Baking time: 20 minutes

A savory tomato sauce tops the crêpes.

FILLING
10 to 12 artichoke hearts, cooked, drained,
   and sliced
2¹/₂ ounces fresh mushrooms, sliced and
   sautéed in butter
2 cups chopped cooked chicken
¹/₂ cup tomato sauce
16 crêpes

1. Combine artichoke hearts, mushrooms, chicken, and tomato sauce. Use about ¹/₄ cup of filling for each crêpe.
2. Fill and roll crêpes. Place in ovenproof covered dish and bake at 350° for 20 minutes.
3. Remove to serving plate, spoon hot sauce (see below) over crêpes and sprinkle with chopped parsley.

SAVORY TOMATO SAUCE
¹/₂ cup chopped onion
2 tablespoons butter
4 cups tomato sauce
1 cup chicken broth
¹/₃ cup water
¹/₃ cup Sauterne or white table wine
3 tablespoons parsley, chopped

1. Sauté onions in butter until they are limp.
2. Add tomato sauce, broth, water, and wine; simmer about 20 minutes. Remove from heat and set aside.

CHICKEN SPINACH CRÊPES

Serves: 12
Temperature: 350°
Baking time: 30 minutes
2 9 x 13 inch pans

FILLING
2 large bunches fresh spinach
4 chicken breasts, cooked
$\frac{1}{2}$ pound mushrooms, sliced
$1\frac{1}{2}$ tablespoons butter
3 green onions, chopped
24 crepes

1. Cook spinach in water that clings to leaves. Drain, squeeze out excess water, and chop.

2. Cut chicken into bite-size pieces.

3. Sauté mushrooms in butter for 2 minutes. Add green onions and sauté 1 minute.

4. Add spinach and chicken.

5. Add just enough cheese sauce (see below) to bind mixture together, reserving remaining sauce. Keep warm on low heat or in double boiler while assembling crêpes.

6. Use $\frac{1}{4}$ cup of filling for each crêpe. Roll and place in oiled pans. Cover with foil and bake at 350° for 30 minutes.

7. Serve on plate or in ramekin (2 per serving); top with some of reserved cheese sauce.

CHEESE SAUCE
4 tablespoons butter, melted
5 tablespoons flour
$2\frac{3}{4}$ cups boiling water
$\frac{1}{4}$ cup heavy cream
1 cup grated Swiss cheese
1 pound (2 packages, 8 ounces each)
cream cheese
Salt and pepper to taste

1. Combine butter and flour in heavy saucepan.

2. Gradually add water, cream, Swiss cheese, and cream cheese.

3. Heat until smooth; season to taste with salt and pepper. Keep warm.

CRÊPES PIPERADE

Serves: 8-10
Temperature: 350°
Baking time: 20 minutes
9 x 13 inch baking dish

2 cups sliced onions
3 tablespoons butter or olive oil
1 pound zucchini, diced
1 green pepper
1 red bell pepper
2 cups fresh tomatoes (peeled, halved,
   seeded, juiced, and sliced)
Salt and pepper to taste
$1/8$ teaspoon each dried thyme, rosemary,
   and oregano, crushed
1 egg, slightly beaten
2 to 3 tablespoons sour cream
8 to 10 crêpes

1. Sauté onions in butter or olive oil in frying pan until translucent, but not browned.
2. Add zucchini, peppers, and tomatoes along with a sprinkling of salt and pepper and the crushed herbs.
3. Toss and stir to blend. Cover pan and cook, stirring several times until peppers are just tender.
4. Uncover pan and boil rapidly to reduce juices to a syrupy consistency.
5. Blend slightly beaten egg with sour cream. Stir into vegetable mixture.
6. Correct seasonings.
7. Fill 8 to 10 crêpes with zucchini mixture, roll, and place in buttered baking dish.
8. Bake in pre-heated 350° oven for 20 minutes.

HAM SPINACH CRÊPES

Serves: 8 (2 crêpes/person)
Temperature: 375°
Baking time: 25 minutes
11 x 14 inch pan

Almost everything can be slip-covered with a crêpe. Here's another classic for leftover baked ham.

1 cup finely chopped onion
1 clove garlic, minced
1 tablespoon oil
2 packages (10 ounces each) frozen chopped
    spinach, thawed and drained well
3 eggs, lightly beaten
2 cups (1 pound) ricotta cheese
1/2 teaspoon salt
1/4 teaspoon nutmeg
1/4 teaspoon pepper
1 teaspoon fresh lemon juice
1/2 cup freshly grated Parmesan cheese
2 cups shredded Monterey Jack cheese
1 cup chopped ham
16 crêpes

1. Sauté onion and garlic in oil until limp. Remove from heat.
2. In large mixing bowl, combine sautéed onion and garlic with the chopped spinach. Stir in lightly beaten eggs, ricotta cheese, salt, nutmeg, pepper, lemon juice, Parmesan cheese, 1 1/2 cups of the Monterey Jack cheese (saving 1/2 cup for the top), and the ham.
3. Mix well and fill crêpes.
4. Place crêpes, seam side down, in oiled pan. Cover with Mornay sauce (*see* below).
5. Top with reserved Jack cheese. Cover with foil.
6. Bake at 375° for 25 minutes.

MORNAY SAUCE
1/2 cup (1 stick) butter
1/2 cup flour
2 cups light cream
2 cups milk
1/2 cup grated Parmesan cheese
Salt and white pepper to taste

1. Melt butter in heavy saucepan; add flour to make a heavy roux.
2. Cook, stirring constantly, until paste bubbles a bit (2 minutes), but do not let it brown.
3. Remove from heat; add cream and milk. Stir well.
4. Put back on heat and stir constantly until mixture thickens.
5. Remove from heat; add Parmesan cheese and salt and pepper to taste.

127

*MANICOTTI CRÊPES

Serves: 8
Temperature: 375°
Baking time: 25 minutes

FILLING
1/2 pound ground pork
1/2 cup chopped onion
1 clove minced garlic
1 package (10 ounces) frozen chopped
   spinach, thawed and drained, or 1 pound
   fresh spinach, cleaned, cooked and
   drained
2 cups ricotta cheese
3 eggs, beaten
1/2 cup chopped parsley
1/4 teaspoon nutmeg
1 cup grated Parmesan cheese
2 cups chopped cooked chicken
1/2 teaspoon salt
3/4 teaspoon pepper
1 cup grated Monterey Jack cheese
16 crêpes

1. In frying pan, cook pork until done. Drain well.

2. Add onion and garlic to pork and sauté until onion is limp.

3. Add spinach, ricotta cheese, eggs, parsley, nutmeg, Parmesan cheese, chicken, salt, and pepper. Mix well.

4. Fill each crêpe with about 1/2 cup filling; roll over and place in shallow baking dish.

5. Cover dish with aluminum foil and bake 25 to 30 minutes at 375° until heated through.

6. To serve, top with heated tomato sauce (see below) and garnish with Monterey Jack cheese.

TOMATO SAUCE
1/3 cup oil
1 large onion, chopped
1 clove garlic, minced
1 can (28 ounces) whole tomatoes
1/8 cup minced parsley
1/2 teaspoon basil
3/4 teaspoon oregano
1/4 teaspoon marjoram
1/2 teaspoon salt
1/2 teaspoon pepper

1. In hot oil in medium saucepan, sauté onion and garlic until limp.

2. Add undrained tomatoes, parsley, basil, oregano, marjoram, salt, and pepper. Mix well, crushing the tomatoes with a fork.

3. Bring to a boil; reduce heat and simmer gently, uncovered, for about 45 minutes.

*CHICKEN MUSHROOM CRÊPES

Serves: 8
Temperature: 375°
Baking time: 15-20 minutes
11 x 14 inch pan

FILLING
$\frac{1}{2}$ cup (1 stick) butter
$\frac{1}{2}$ cup chopped onion
1 cup sliced celery
$\frac{1}{2}$ teaspoon salt
$\frac{1}{4}$ teaspoon pepper
1 pound fresh mushrooms, sliced
$2\frac{1}{2}$ cups chopped cooked chicken
2 tablespoons dry sherry
1 cup green-ripe olives, sliced
1 cup Mornay sauce (see below)
1 cup grated Monterey Jack cheese
16 crêpes

1. In a large saucepan, melt butter, sauté onion and celery. Season with salt and pepper.
2. Add mushrooms and cook 2 to 3 minutes, stirring occasionally.
3. Add chicken, sherry, and olives. Stir well.
4. Add half of the Mornay sauce. Cook over low heat until mixture is well blended. Cool slightly.
5. Fill and roll crêpes. Place in buttered baking dish.
6. Cover with remaining Mornay sauce and the shredded Monterey Jack cheese. Bake at 375° for 15 to 20 minutes.

MORNAY SAUCE
$\frac{1}{4}$ cup (4 tablespoons) butter
$\frac{1}{2}$ cup flour
$\frac{1}{2}$ teaspoon salt
$\frac{1}{4}$ teaspoon pepper
$1\frac{3}{4}$ cups chicken broth
$\frac{3}{4}$ cup light cream
1 cup grated Monterey Jack cheese

1. Make a roux of flour, butter, salt, and pepper.
2. Stir in chicken broth and light cream.
3. Cook over medium heat, stirring constantly until thickened.
4. Add grated Jack cheese.
5. Stir constantly until cheese is melted.

RATATOUILLE CRÊPES

Serves: 5
Temperature: 350°
Baking time: 30 minutes
9 x 13 inch pan

You prepare the sauce a day ahead so seasonings can get well acquainted.

FILLING
1½ cups sliced fresh mushrooms
3 green onions with tops, thinly sliced
2 tablespoons butter
2 medium-size zucchini, thinly sliced
½ cup chopped bell pepper
1 large tomato, peeled, halved, seeded,
    and chopped
½ cup grated Parmesan cheese
¼ teaspoon dried marjoram
¼ teaspoon dried thyme
½ teaspoon dried basil
10 crêpes
1 cup grated Swiss cheese
Grated Swiss cheese and Monterey Jack
    cheese for garnish

1. Sauté mushrooms and green onion in butter until juices evaporate.

2. Add zucchini and bell pepper and cook 10 minutes. Do not cover.

3. Add tomato, Parmesan cheese, and seasonings.

4. Place ¼ cup of mixture on each crêpe. Sprinkle each with about 1½ tablespoons of the grated Swiss cheese.

5. Roll crêpes and place seam side down in oiled 9 x 13 inch pan. Cover and bake at 350° for 30 minutes. Reheat tomato sauce.

6. Pour hot tomato sauce over crêpes (figure on 2 per serving) and sprinkle tops with grated Swiss and Monterey Jack cheese.

TOMATO SAUCE
1 cup chopped onion
3 tablespoons oil
¼ cup Sauterne
1 can (15 ounces) tomato sauce
1 cup water
¼ cup dried parsley

1. Sauté onion in oil until limp and golden.

2. Add wine, tomato sauce, water, and parsley; simmer until thick. Refrigerate.

CALIFORNIA CASSEROLE

Serves: 12-14
Temperature: 350°
Baking time: 1 hour
3 quart casserole

This dish should be made ahead and refrigerated until 1 hour before serving to a crowd.

2 pounds ground chuck
¼ cup olive oil
1 cup chopped onion
1 clove garlic, minced
½ cup chopped green pepper
1 can (16 ounces) tomatoes (2 cups)
1 can (8 ounces) tomato sauce
1 can (12 ounces) whole kernel corn
1 tablespoon salt
1 tablespoon chili powder
1 teaspoon cumin
¼ teaspoon black pepper
1 cup water
½ cup corn meal
1 cup pitted ripe olives, sliced

1. Brown ground chuck in olive oil. Add onion, garlic, and green pepper, and stir until onion is golden.

2. Add tomatoes, tomato sauce, corn, salt, chili powder, cumin, and black pepper. Simmer for 15 minutes.

3. Mix together water and corn meal and add to meat mixture. Cover and simmer 15 minutes.

4. Add ripe olives. Put mixture into 3 quart casserole dish. Top with spoon bread (see below) and refrigerate until 1 hour before serving time.

5. Bake at 350° for 1 hour.

SPOON BREAD
1½ cups milk
1 teaspoon salt
2 tablespoons butter
½ cup corn meal
1 cup grated Cheddar cheese
2 eggs, slightly beaten

1. In saucepan heat milk, salt, and butter over low heat.

2. Slowly stir in corn meal and cook, stirring constantly, until thick.

3. Remove from heat and stir in cheese and slightly beaten eggs. Mix well and pour over meat mixture.

131

FETTUCINE WITH ARTICHOKES AND ITALIAN SAUSAGE

Serves: 6

For a nice change of pace, use green fettucine in this instead of the usual white.

4 sweet Italian sausages (about ³/₄ pound),
    casings removed and the meat crumbled
1 large onion, chopped
2 cloves garlic, minced
30 egg-size fresh artichokes, trimmed into
    hearts, quartered, and soaked in
    acidulated water
¹/₂ cup dry white table wine
1 cup chicken stock or canned chicken broth
³/₄ pound uncooked fettucine
¹/₄ cup (¹/₂ stick) unsalted butter, softened
¹/₃ cup freshly grated Parmesan cheese
2 tablespoons minced fresh parsley leaves

1. In a large stainless steel or enameled skillet, sauté the sausage over moderately high heat until it is browned.

2. Add the onion and garlic, and cook the mixture over moderate heat, stirring, until the onion is golden.

3. Add the quartered artichoke hearts, well drained, wine, and stock. Bring the liquid to a boil and simmer the mixture, covered, for 15 to 20 minutes, or until the artichoke hearts are just tender.

4. Remove cover and cook, stirring occasionally, for 8 to 10 minutes, or until the juices have thickened slightly. Keep warm, covered.

5. In a kettle of boiling salted water, cook the fettucine until it is al dente, drain, and transfer to a heated bowl.

6. Toss the fettucine with the butter, the artichoke mixture, and salt and pepper to taste. Sprinkle the mixture with the Parmesan and the parsley.

7. Serve immediately on hot plates.

*SPINACH LASAGNE WITH MORNAY SAUCE

Serves: 12
Temperature: 350°
Baking time: 30 minutes
9 x 13 inch pan

MORNAY SAUCE
4 tablespoons butter
4 tablespoons flour
3 cups light cream
³/₄ teaspoon salt
³/₈ teaspoon nutmeg
1¹/₂ cups Parmesan cheese

1. Melt butter and stir in flour.
2. Gradually add light cream, stirring until thickened. Season with salt, nutmeg, and cheese.

FILLING
2 pounds well-washed fresh spinach,
   stems removed
1 medium onion, chopped
1 rib celery, finely sliced
¹/₂ pound mushrooms, sliced
2 cloves garlic, minced
2 tablespoons butter
³/₄ teaspoon seasoning salt
¹/₈ teaspoon pepper
³/₄ cup chopped walnuts
1¹/₂ teaspoons dry basil
1¹/₂ teaspoons marjoram
9 lasagne noodles
2 cups shredded Monterey Jack cheese
¹/₄ cup grated Parmesan cheese

1. Cook spinach, in the water droplets left on the leaves from washing, until just wilted. Turn spinach into strainer and firmly press out excess moisture with large spoon. Turn out onto chopping board and chop fine.
2. Sauté onion, celery, mushrooms, and garlic in butter.
3. Combine spinach, seasoning salt, pepper, walnuts, and herbs. Remove from heat.
4. Cook noodles according to package directions.
5. In 9 x 13 inch baking dish spread small amount of Mornay sauce, then layer ingredients as follows: 3 lasagne noodles, ¹/₂ of the filling, 1 cup sauce. Repeat with 3 noodles, remaining filling, 1 cup sauce. Add another layer of 3 noodles and spread remaining sauce over top.
6. Sprinkle 2 cups of shredded Monterey Jack cheese and the ¹/₄ cup of Parmesan cheese over the casserole.
7. Bake at 350°, covered, for 30 minutes or until hot and bubbly. Then bake uncovered for 5 minutes.

MALFATTI WITH TOMATO MEAT SAUCE

Serves: 6-8

The tomato meat sauce may be prepared the day before serving with the Malfatti. Serve with a green salad, French bread, and red wine.

MALFATTI
1 cup cooked spinach (approximately)
　　(1 package 10 ounces frozen spinach,
　　thoroughly defrosted, squeezed dry, and
　　chopped; or 1$^1/_2$ pounds fresh spinach,
　　cooked, drained, squeezed dry,
　　and chopped)
1$^1/_2$ cups ricotta cheese
1 cup fine dry bread crumbs
2 eggs, beaten
$^3/_4$ cup grated Parmesan cheese
$^1/_4$ cup finely diced onions
1 large clove garlic, minced
1 tablespoon finely-cut fresh basil or
　　1 teaspoon dry basil
$^1/_4$ teaspoon nutmeg

1. Combine the spinach, ricotta cheese, bread crumbs, beaten eggs, $^1/_4$ cup of the Parmesan cheese, finely diced onions, garlic, and seasonings. Chill this mixture until it is firm enough to shape.

2. Form into 1$^1/_2$ inch "fingers." Roll lightly in flour. Place in single layer on cookie sheet. Cover with plastic wrap and chill thoroughly.

3. Poach the Malfatti, a few at a time, in a large skillet of simmering water. They will rise to surface of water when cooked. Remove with slotted spoon to serving platter.

4. Top with hot tomato-meat sauce (see below) and sprinkle with the remaining $^1/_2$ cup of Parmesan cheese. Serve at once.

Continued...

TOMATO MEAT SAUCE
$^1/_2$ pound lean ground beef
2 tablespoons olive oil
1 cup chopped onion
2 cloves garlic, chopped
2$^1/_2$ cups canned plum tomatoes,
    undrained
1 can (6 ounces) tomato paste
2 cups beef broth
1 bay leaf
$^1/_2$ teaspoon salt
$^1/_4$ teaspoon freshly ground pepper
1 tablespoon finely-cut fresh basil or
    1 teaspoon dried basil
$^1/_2$ teaspoon dried oregano

1. Brown meat in olive oil. Add onion and garlic and continue cooking until onions are soft, stirring often.
2. Add the tomatoes, tomato paste, beef broth, bay leaf, seasonings, and herbs. Simmer, uncovered, stirring occasionally, about 2 hours. Add more water as necessary.
3. Remove the bay leaf. Taste for seasoning.

ZUCCHINI LASAGNE

Serves: 8-10
Temperature: 350°
Baking time: 35-40 minutes
9 x 13 inch pan

1 pound ground beef
½ cup chopped onion
1 can (16 ounces) tomato puree
1 teaspoon garlic salt
1 teaspoon garlic powder
1 teaspoon dried oregano leaves
Freshly ground pepper
1½ cups (12 ounces) ricotta cheese
½ cup Parmesan cheese
1 egg
1½ pounds medium-sized zucchini
½ pound mozzarella cheese, sliced
or grated

1. Brown beef with onion; drain fat. Stir in tomato puree, garlic salt, garlic powder, oregano, and pepper. Simmer, covered, for 10 minutes, stirring occasionally.

2. Combine ricotta cheese, ¼ cup of the Parmesan cheese, and egg.

3. Wash zucchini and remove ends; slice lengthwise as thin as possible, about ⅛ inch.

4. In a 9 x 13 inch oiled pan, layer ingredients as follows: half of the zucchini; all of the ricotta cheese mixture; half of the mozzarella cheese; half of the meat sauce.

5. Repeat above except for ricotta cheese mixture. Sprinkle top with the remaining Parmesan cheese.

6. Bake, uncovered, 35 to 40 minutes at 350°.

7. Remove from oven and let stand 10 minutes before cutting.

POLENTA WITH QUAIL

Serves: 4

4 quail
2 tablespoons oil
¹/₂ cup chopped onion
¹/₂ cup chopped celery
¹/₄ cup chopped carrot
¹/₂ pound mushrooms, sliced
1 clove garlic, minced
¹/₂ cup dry white table wine
1 can (8 ounces) tomato sauce
1 cup water
¹/₂ teaspoon sage leaves, crumbled
Salt and pepper to taste

1. Brown quail in oil in a large, heavy skillet. When nicely browned, transfer to a casserole and cover to keep warm.
2. Sauté onion, celery, carrot, mushrooms, and garlic in same skillet until limp.
3. Add wine and cook for about 1 minute.
4. Add tomato sauce, water, sage, and salt and pepper. Taste for seasonings.
5. Cook sauce at medium heat for about 5 minutes.
6. Return quail to sauce and simmer for about 20 minutes. Do not overcook. Serve with polenta (see below).

POLENTA
6¹/₂ cups water
1 tablespoon salt
2 cups coarse-ground cornmeal

1. Bring water to boil in a large, heavy kettle.
2. Add salt and reduce heat to medium-low so the water is just simmering.
3. Add cornmeal in a very thin stream, stirring with a stout, long wooden spoon. Stir continuously, keeping the water at a slow, steady simmer.
4. Continue stirring for 20 minutes after all of the cornmeal has been added. The polenta is done when it tears away from the sides of the pot as you stir.
5. Pour the polenta onto a large platter and arrange the quail on top of polenta. Cover with sauce and serve immediately.

CHICKEN CHEESE ENCHILADAS

Serves: 9-12
Temperature: 350°
Baking time: 25 minutes
2 9 x 13 inch pans

You bite into these enchiladas and discover cubes of chicken surrounded by both Cheddar and Jack cheeses.

2 cans (1 pound 12 ounces each) whole
   tomatoes
$1/2$ teaspoon paprika
6 teaspoons chili powder
$1/2$ teaspoon cumin powder
2 teaspoons oregano, crushed
$1/2$ teaspoon salt
2 cloves garlic, minced
2 onions, chopped fine
Oil for frying
4 cups grated Cheddar cheese
3 cups grated Monterey Jack cheese
12 flour tortillas OR 18 corn tortillas
3 cooked whole chicken breasts, skinned,
   boned, and chopped into $1/2$ inch cubes
Chopped green chilies to taste (optional)
Grated Parmesan cheese

1. In a saucepan, mix together tomatoes, paprika, chili powder, cumin, oregano, and salt. Simmer until thick, about 45 minutes to 1 hour.

2. Strain and press tomato mixture through sieve, removing all juice.

3. Sauté garlic and onions in oil and add to thick, strained sauce.

4. In a bowl, mix together Cheddar and Jack cheeses.

5. If using <u>flour</u> tortillas, dip each tortilla in thick tomato sauce before filling. Place $1/2$ cup of cheese mixture in center of tortilla; add 5 to 6 pieces of chicken cubes and, if desired, chopped green chilies. Top with 1 tablespoon thick tomato sauce.

6. If using <u>corn</u> tortillas, heat each tortilla in hot oil in fry pan for a few seconds, just until softened. Dip into thick tomato sauce; fill as with flour tortillas, using smaller quantities of filling.

7. Cover bottom of 9 x 13 inch pans with tomato sauce. Roll enchiladas and place, seam side down, in dishes. Sprinkle tortillas with remaining cheese mixture; top with grated Parmesan cheese.

8. Bake at 350° for 25 minutes.

ENCHILADA BURRITOS

Serves: 12
Temperature: 350°
Baking time: 35-45 minutes
2 9 x 12 inch pans

1½ pounds ground beef
2 teaspoons flour
¼ teaspoon sugar
½ teaspoon seasoned salt
1 clove garlic, minced
¼ teaspoon cumin
¼ teaspoon dry red chili flakes
4 teaspoons chili powder
1 can (8 ounces) tomato sauce
1 cup water
1 can (29 ounces) pinto beans, undrained
1 can (29 ounces) red chili sauce
1 dozen flour tortillas
6 hard-cooked eggs, chopped
1 large onion, chopped
1 pound Cheddar cheese, grated

1. Brown ground beef and drain off excess fat well.
2. Mix flour, sugar, and seasonings. Add to browned beef.
3. Add tomato sauce, water, and pinto beans. Simmer 30 minutes.
4. Drain any liquid from meat mixture into red chili sauce.
5. Spread a few spoonfuls of sauce on each tortilla before topping with meat mixture, chopped hard-cooked egg, chopped onion, and grated cheese.
6. Roll tortillas and place in buttered baking pan.
7. Cover with red chili sauce and any remaining cheese.
8. Bake at 350° for 35 to 45 minutes.

ENCHILADAS MOLE VERDE

Serves: 8
Temperature: 400°
Baking time: 25 minutes
9 x 13 x 2 inch baking dish

MOLE VERDE
1 medium-sized onion, finely chopped
¼ cup finely chopped blanched almonds
2 tablespoons salad oil
**2 cans (10 ounces each) tomatillos,
    undrained**
**1 tablespoon fresh minced coriander or 1
    teaspoon dry ground coriander**
**3 chopped green jalapeño peppers with seeds
    and pith removed**
2 cups chicken broth

1. Combine the onion, almonds, and salad oil in a saucepan.
2. Cook, stirring, over moderate heat until onion is soft and the almonds are lightly browned.
3. Whirl the tomatillos and liquid in a blender until mixture is fairly smooth; add to onion and almond mixture.
4. Stir in the coriander and jalapeños.
5. Add the chicken broth and simmer rapidly, uncovered, until reduced to 2½ cups; stir occasionally.
6. Sauce may be made ahead and refrigerated, then reheated when ready to assemble the enchiladas.

Continued...

ENCHILADAS
¹/₂ pound sharp Cheddar cheese, grated
1 pound Monterey Jack cheese, grated
3 cans (4 ounces each) diced green chilies
1 large onion, chopped
4 hard cooked eggs, chopped
18 corn tortillas
2 cups sour cream

1. Mix cheeses, except for ¹/₂ cup set aside, with chiles, onion, and chopped eggs.

2. Reheat sauce.

3. Dip fresh tortillas in small amount of heated Mole Verde sauce to soften slightly before assembling.

4. Fill each tortilla with about ¹/₃ cup of cheese mixture; roll the tortilla and place seam side down in a greased baking dish.

5. Cover enchiladas with remainder of the Mole Verde sauce.

6. Sprinkle on top, the ¹/₂ cup cheese set aside.

7. Cover and bake in 400° oven until hot and bubbly, about 25 minutes.

8. Remove from oven, remove cover, and let set until ready to serve with sour cream. (These are best when allowed to "set up" for a little while.)

ENCHILADAS DEL RANCHO

Serves: 6
Temperature: 350°
Baking time: 15 minutes
9 x 13 inch greased baking dish

ENCHILADA SAUCE
1 can (15 ounces) tomato sauce
$\frac{1}{2}$ cup water
$2\frac{1}{2}$ teaspoons chili powder
$\frac{1}{2}$ teaspoon salt
$\frac{1}{2}$ teaspoon garlic powder
$\frac{1}{4}$ teaspoon cumin

1. Combine tomato sauce with water and seasonings. Simmer for 20 minutes.
2. Before serving, top each enchilada with a dollop of sour cream and a few slices of stuffed green olives.

ENCHILADAS
Oil for softening tortillas
12 large corn tortillas
1 cup sour cream
4 sliced green onions
$1\frac{1}{2}$ cups small-curd low-fat cottage cheese
1 can (4 ounces) diced green chilies,
   not drained
$\frac{1}{2}$ cup sliced stuffed green olives (reserve
   a few slices for garnish)
3 cups grated Monterey Jack cheese (reserve
   a little for top)
Sour cream for garnish

1. In large frying pan, heat small amount of oil and fry each tortilla on both sides just long enough to soften (30 seconds). Drain on paper towels. Set aside.
2. In a bowl, mix sour cream, green onions, cottage cheese, green chilies, and green olives.
3. Spoon $\frac{1}{4}$ cup of mixture onto each tortilla and add a sprinkling of the grated cheese. Roll up tortillas and place, seam side down, in greased baking dish.
4. Spoon enchilada sauce over filled tortillas. Cover and bake at 350° for 15 minutes or until heated through. Just before serving top with remaining grated cheese and put under broiler until cheese melts.

ENCHILADAS BETH

This recipe comes from John Steinbeck's sister.

Las Palmas enchilada sauce—plus some Las Palmas red-hot sauce (for 24, I use two 1-pound cans plus about 1 cup hot sauce, or to taste). Add salt, pepper, a little cumin if desired, one large clove garlic, and one large tablespoon lard or Crisco. Brown some flour and thicken the sauce slightly with it.

Be sure pan is big enough around so that tortillas can lie flat and be removed easily.

Fry flour tortillas quickly in lard—one at a time while making enchilada—drain, put in hot sauce for a minute or two and then place on a dinner plate. I use flat spatula to lift tortilla in and out of pan, and leave it under it while on the plate being filled.

To each tortilla in center:

1 large tablespoon steamed chopped onion
1/2 chopped hard-cooked egg
1 tablespoon mixed green and black olives
  (chopped)
1 large tablespoon grated sharp Cheddar
  cheese

Place some hot sauce in flat pan, close tortilla, over the filling, and place upside down in flat pan. Place more cheese, olives and sauce on each.

Bake about 15 minutes at 400° or until cheese is all melted and sauce is bubbling.

This is a messy job—use lots of newspapers. I get all filling ready, each in a large bowl, then begin on the sauce. Roll my table to the stove—have pans nearby and ready. Good luck.

©Steve Crouch

Side Dishes

These unusual side dishes provide varied and interesting substitutes for more conventional menu items. Recipes include recommendations as to how the side dish can best be used.

GNOCCHI ALLA ROMANA

Serves: 4—6
Temperature: 400°
Baking time: 15 minutes
Large baking sheet; 8 or 9 inch
*   shallow baking dish*

A wonderful change from the more usual pasta.

3 cups milk
1½ teaspoons salt
Pinch of ground nutmeg
Freshly ground black pepper
¾ cup semolina or farina
2 eggs
1 cup freshly grated Parmesan cheese,
**   divided**
4 tablespoons butter, melted

1. Grease a large baking sheet and set aside.

2. In a heavy 2 to 3 quart saucepan, bring the milk, salt, nutmeg, and a few grindings of pepper to a boil over moderate heat.

3. Add the semolina or farina gradually, so the milk never stops boiling, stirring constantly with a wooden spoon. Continue cooking and stirring until the mixture is so thick that the spoon will stand unsupported in the middle of the pan. Remove from heat.

4. Beat eggs lightly with a fork, mix with ¾ cup of the Parmesan cheese, and stir into the semolina.

5. When the ingredients are well blended, spoon the mixture onto the greased baking sheet.

6. Using a metal spatula, which should be dipped in hot water from time to time to make the semolina easier to handle, smooth and spread the semolina into a sheet about ¼ inch thick. Refrigerate for at least 1 hour or until semolina is firm.

7. Preheat oven to 400° and butter an 8 or 9 inch shallow baking and serving dish.

8. Cut the semolina with a 1½ inch biscuit cutter (or use a sharp knife to cut into triangles).

9. Transfer the shapes to the baking dish, dribble with the melted butter, and sprinkle the tops with the remaining ¼ cup of Parmesan cheese.

10. Bake the gnocchi on the middle shelf of the oven for 15 minutes or until they are crisp and golden. You may brown the tops by placing them under a hot broiler for 30 seconds.

11. Serve the gnocchi at once, while they are hot.

PASTA AND BROCCOLI VINAIGRETTE

Serves: 4-6
Large cooking pot

1 bunch broccoli, trimmed, peeled, and cut
   into 3 to 4 inch pieces (about 2½ cups raw)
8 ounces uncooked spaghetti
¼ cup olive oil
¼ cup vegetable oil
¼ cup cider vinegar
1 clove garlic, minced
1½ teaspoons salt
1 teaspoon dried basil
¼ teaspoon liquid hot pepper
2 green onions, thinly sliced
3 fresh tomatoes, quartered (or you can use
   cherry tomatoes)

1. Cook spaghetti and broccoli together in boiling salted water for 10 minutes.

2. Drain thoroughly and keep hot.

3. While spaghetti and broccoli are cooking, combine oils, vinegar, garlic, basil, liquid hot pepper, green onions, and salt in a saucepan and bring to a boil over medium heat, stirring constantly.

4. Immediately pour over drained and warm pasta and broccoli and garnish with tomatoes.

5. Serve immediately.

WILD WEST RICE

Serves: 8
Temperature: 325°
Baking time: 30-35 minutes
9 x 13 inch baking dish

1 clove garlic, chopped fine
1 medium-size green pepper, chopped
1 medium-size onion, chopped
¹/₂ cup minced parsley
¹/₂ cup green chilies, seeded, rinsed and diced
1 cup grated sharp Cheddar cheese
1 small package (3 ounces) cream cheese,
  softened
1 tablespoon pimiento, chopped
1 tablespoon butter
¹/₄ pound fresh mushrooms, sliced
2 cups cooked rice
2 eggs, beaten
1 teaspoon salt
³/₄ cup light cream

1. In a medium bowl combine garlic, green pepper, onion, parsley, chilies, and Cheddar cheese.

2. In small bowl cream together pimiento and cream cheese.

3. Melt butter in skillet. Sauté mushrooms for 1 minute.

4. Stir in the cream cheese-pimento mixture and cooked rice. Add Cheddar cheese mixture. Mix well. Place in 9 x 13 inch buttered pan. (At this point the dish may be refrigerated overnight.)

5. Just before baking, mix together eggs, salt, and light cream and pour over the rice mixture.

6. Bake at 325° for 30 to 35 minutes or until lightly browned and set. Watch your time!

WILD RICE AND MUSHROOMS

Serves: 8
Temperature: 350°
Baking time: 1 hour
2¹/₂ quart casserole

This festive dish is excellent with game, roasts and baked or barbecued salmon.

1 cup (6 ounces) wild rice
1 cup chopped onion
3 tablespoons butter, divided
³/₄ pound mushrooms, sliced
¹/₄ pound (1 stick) butter, melted
4 cloves garlic, pressed
Salt and pepper

1. Wash rice well. Cover with 2 inches cold, unsalted water. Boil gently for 30 minutes or until nearly tender. Drain.

2. Put rice in colander or steamer; place over boiling water. Cover with tea towel and steam until done, 10 to 15 minutes.

3. Put rice in casserole, salt lightly.

4. In large skillet, sauté onion in one tablespoon of the butter until limp. Remove from pan and set aside.

5. In same pan, sauté mushrooms in the remaining 2 tablespoons of the butter until lightly browned. Add prepared rice, stir, and sauté for a few minutes.

6. Turn rice mixture into casserole, add sautéed onion, and stir to mix. If desired, refrigerate mixture.

7. One hour before serving, pour over rice the ¹/₄ pound melted butter to which the pressed garlic has been added. Stir and taste for salt and pepper.

8. Reheat, covered, in 350° oven for 1 hour.

*PEARL BARLEY WITH MUSHROOMS

Serves: 8
Temperature: 350°
Baking time: 1 to 1¼ hours
1 quart baking dish

½ cup onions, chopped
3 tablespoons butter
1 cup uncooked pearl barley
3 cups regular-strength chicken stock
½ pound mushrooms, sliced
2 tablespoons butter
1 teaspoon salt
¼ teaspoon pepper

1. Sauté onions in the butter until transparent.

2. Stir in pearl barley and cook 3 to 5 minutes or until lightly browned.

3. Add chicken broth; bring to a boil.

4. Cook, covered, in 350° oven for 1 hour.

5. Meanwhile, sauté mushrooms in the 2 tablespoons butter; season with salt and pepper. Add to barley (at end of 1 hour) and cook another 15 minutes.

6. Let stand a few minutes before serving.

KANSAS GRITS

Serves: 8 to 10
Temperature: 350°
Baking time: 1 hour
2 quart souffle dish

Use in place of rice or potatoes; great for barbecue!

1¼ cups quick-cooking hominy grits
6 cups boiling water
2 teaspoons salt
1 pound sharp Cheddar cheese, grated*
¼ pound (1 stick) butter
3 to 4 drops hot pepper sauce
3 eggs, beaten
Paprika

1. Slowly stir grits into boiling salt water. Reduce heat to low, cover, and cook 5 to 6 minutes or until thick, stirring occasionally. Remove from heat.

2. Add cheese, butter, hot pepper sauce, and beaten eggs. Mix thoroughly and pour into buttered souffle dish.

3. Bake, uncovered, at 350° for 1 hour. Sprinkle top with paprika 10 minutes before done.

4. Remove from oven and let stand for 15 to 20 minutes before serving.

   *Sharp Cheddar cheese is essential because we found other cheeses too bland.

JOHN'S POTATO DISH

3 slices bacon, cut in 1 inch squares
3 medium potatoes, coarsely grated
2 medium onions, chopped
$1/2$ teaspoon salt
$1/4$ teaspoon pepper
$1/4$ teaspoon poultry seasoning
1 small can evaporated milk

1. Sauté bacon in heavy skillet to cover bottom with bacon drippings.

2. Mix potatoes, onions, seasonings, and spread evenly in skillet.

3. Pour milk over all. Do not mix.

4. Cover and cook over medium-low heat for at least 30 minutes. This can stay on very low heat for an hour and a half or more.

When the conversation was more interesting than coming to table, John Steinbeck used to turn down the heat on his special potato dish which ended up tasting better and better...remembered from the 30's—Virginia Scardigli.

BAKED ONIONS

Serves: 8
Temperature: 350°
Baking time: $1^{1}/_{4}$ hours
Shallow baking pan

This dish goes well with steak, roasts or Thanksgiving turkey.

4 large yellow onions
4 teaspoons butter
$1/2$ teaspoon garlic salt
$1/2$ teaspoon black pepper
1 teaspoon instant beef bouillon crystals
$1/2$ cup dried bread crumbs
$1/2$ cup grated Parmesan cheese

1. Cut ends off onions, peel and cut in half crosswise, making slices about 1 inch thick.

2. Place in single layer in shallow baking pan and put $1/2$ teaspoon butter on each half.

3. Mix garlic salt, black pepper, and bouillon; sprinkle $1/4$ teaspoon of mixture over each half.

4. Bake, covered, for 1 hour at 350.°

5. Mix bread crumbs and Parmesan cheese and sprinkle 1 tablespoon over each half.

6. Bake, uncovered, for 15 minutes more.

7. Serve one-half per person.

©Steve Crouch

Vegetables

The Steinbeck House kitchen uses only fresh vegetables from the fields of the Salinas Valley. Vegetables are elevated from the mundane when they are tasty Cointreau Carrots or Zucchini Chaos.

SPANISH SQUASH

Serves: 8 as a main dish
10-12 as side dish
Temperature: 350°
Baking time: 30-35 minutes
9 x 13 inch pan

This dish is especially nice for brunch.

2 pounds zucchini, sliced thinly
¼ pound (1 stick) butter
1 cup dry bread crumbs
4 eggs
2 teaspoons baking powder
3 tablespoons flour
1 can (7 ounces) green chilies, seeded
  and chopped
1 pound Monterey Jack cheese, grated
Dash of garlic salt
2 tablespoons chopped parsley
1 cup peeled, seeded and chopped tomatoes

1. Boil sliced squash in 1 cup water for 5 minutes; drain well.
2. Melt butter in baking pan in preheated oven. Stir in bread crumbs; mix well. Take out ½ cup buttered crumbs and reserve for topping. Spread remainder evenly in pan.
3. Beat eggs slightly with baking powder, flour, and garlic salt. Gently stir in chilies, grated cheese, parsley, tomatoes, and drained zucchini slices.
4. Spread evenly in crumb-lined pan; top with remaining buttered crumbs.
5. Bake 30 to 35 minutes in moderate oven (350°) or until set and lightly browned. Let stand 5 minutes before serving, to set custard.

ARTICHOKE SAUTÉ

Serves: 4

This can be made ahead and reheated.

> ¹/₄ cup olive oil
> 10 to 12 baby artichokes (jumbo egg size),
>   trimmed, quartered
> 2 garlic cloves, minced
> ¹/₄ cup parsley, chopped
> 1 teaspoon Italian herb seasoning
> Salt and pepper
> 1 cup dry white table wine

1. Heat oil in a large skillet. Add quartered artichokes and sauté briefly on all sides.

2. Stir in garlic, parsley, herb seasoning, and wine.

3. Cover and simmer until artichokes are tender but still crunchy, about 15 to 20 minutes.

FIESTA CELERY AND CARROTS

Serves: 4-6
2 quart saucepan

> 3 tablespoons salad oil or butter
> 1 cup chopped onions
> ¹/₂ cup chopped green peppers
> 1 clove garlic, minced
> 2 cups sliced carrots
> 2 cups sliced celery (¹/₂ inch slices)
> ¹/₂ teaspoon salt
> ¹/₄ teaspoon pepper
> ¹/₄ teaspoon oregano
> 1 teaspoon liquid hot pepper sauce
> 1 can (8 ounces) tomato sauce
> ¹/₄ cup water

1. Heat oil in 2 quart saucepan; stir in onion, green peppers, and garlic.

2. Cook until soft but not brown.

3. Add carrots, celery, and seasonings; bring to a boil.

4. Simmer, covered, about 20 to 30 minutes, until tender.

GREEN BEAN BUNDLES

Serves: 6

1 pound fresh green beans
2 tablespoons butter
1 small clove garlic, minced
1 small package (4 ounces) thinly sliced,
    fully-cooked ham, julienned
$1/4$ teaspoon salt
Dash of pepper
12 to 14 small cherry tomatoes, halved

1. Trim beans, leave whole and tie with string in 6 equal bundles.

2. Cook quickly in boiling water until barely tender; drain. Plunge into cold water and drain again.

3. Melt butter in saucepan and add garlic and slivered ham. Cook over low heat until garlic is softened.

4. Place bean bundles on serving platter; remove strings but keep bundles separated. Arrange julienned ham over beans lengthwise.

5. Add salt, pepper, and halved tomatoes to garlic butter and pour mixture over beans and ham.

156

HERBED GREEN BEANS

These green beans are well seasoned but the beans don't lose their identity.

1^1/$_2$ **pounds green beans**
^{1}/$_4$ **cup (^{1}/$_2$ stick) butter**
^{1}/$_3$ **cup finely chopped onion**
^{1}/$_3$ **cup finely sliced celery**
^{1}/$_2$ **clove garlic, crushed**
^{1}/$_4$ **teaspoon dried basil**
^{1}/$_4$ **teaspoon dried rosemary**
^{1}/$_4$ **teaspoon dried summer savory**
^{1}/$_2$ **teaspoon salt**

1. Break off tips and thinly slice green beans.
2. In saucepan, melt butter and sauté onion, celery, and garlic until onion is tender but not browned.
3. Stir in the green beans, herbs, and salt.
4. Cover the saucepan and cook over low heat for 15 minutes, or until beans are tender.

For a novel vegetable dish, add strips of fresh pear to cooked green beans—a color, texture, and flavor contrast. Don't cook the pears; just add them at the last minute to heat through. Diced pears may be added to green peas in the same way.

SESAME GLAZED BROCCOLI

Serves: 4

1 tablespoon sesame seeds
1 tablespoon vegetable oil
1 tablespoon chopped sweet onion
2 tablespoons chopped fresh carrot
4 cups washed and trimmed broccoli
   flowerets
$\frac{1}{4}$ cup dry white table wine
$\frac{1}{2}$ cup chicken broth
$\frac{1}{4}$ teaspoon salt
$\frac{1}{4}$ teaspoon pepper
1 tablespoon arrowroot or cornstarch

1. Toast sesame seeds in small pie tin in 350° oven until brown (about 5 minutes). Set aside.

2. Heat oil in large saucepan over medium heat. Stir in onion and carrot and sauté until soft (about 3 to 4 minutes).

3. Add broccoli flowerets, wine, chicken broth, salt, and pepper.

4. Cook, partially covered, over medium-high heat, stirring occasionally until broccoli is just tender (about 8 to 10 minutes).

5. Remove vegetables with a slotted spoon and place in serving bowl, leaving liquid in the saucepan.

6. Stir arrowroot into liquid, and cook over medium heat until slightly thickened.

7. Add toasted sesame seeds and pour sauce over broccoli. Serve at once.

BROCCOLI GRUYERE

Serves: 4-6

$1\frac{1}{2}$ to 2 pounds fresh broccoli
3 tablespoons butter
2 tablespoons flour
$\frac{1}{4}$ cup milk
Salt to taste
$\frac{1}{8}$ teaspoon pepper
$\frac{1}{2}$ cup shredded Gruyere cheese
2 tablespoons fine, dry bread crumbs

1. Cut broccoli in spears, peel stems, and cook until barely tender; drain, reserving $\frac{1}{2}$ cup of the liquid.
2. Arrange broccoli in a greased, shallow heat-proof dish; set aside and keep warm.
3. Melt butter and blend in flour. Stir in reserved liquid from broccoli and the milk. Cook and stir until thickened.
4. Season with salt and pepper.
5. Pour sauce over broccoli. Sprinkle with Gruyere cheese, then bread crumbs.
6. Broil about 8 inches from heat until golden brown.

Try a fluffy cheese sauce with broccoli, cauliflower, or brussels sprouts. Melt $\frac{1}{4}$ cup butter, add $\frac{1}{4}$ cup flour, then stir in 2 cups milk. When thickened, get out your mixer and beat in one pound processed cheese. Still beating, add about half a can of beer, 1 tablespoon prepared mustard, and 1 tablespoon Worcestershire. Keep beating until fluffy.

SPRING VEGETABLE SKILLET

Serves: 5-6
Large, heavy skillet

1 small head cauliflower, broken into
   flowerets (2½ to 3 cups)
1 cup water
⅓ cup butter
2 cups sliced zucchini
1 medium-size green pepper, cut into strips
   2 x ½ inch
¼ cup chopped sweet onion
½ teaspoon salt
1 teaspoon dried basil
1 teaspoon dried oregano
1 clove garlic, crushed
¼ teaspoon ground pepper
2 medium-size tomatoes, each cut into
   8 wedges
3 tablespoons butter
3 tablespoons freshly grated Parmesan
   cheese

1. In skillet, combine cauliflower and water. Bring to a boil and cook, covered, 5 minutes or until barely tender. Drain.

2. Add butter, zucchini, green pepper, onion, salt, basil, oregano, garlic, and ground pepper. Cook, uncovered, over medium heat, tossing occasionally, until zucchini is tender-crisp.

3. Add tomatoes, butter, and Parmesan cheese. Remove from heat and toss until blended. Serve immediately.

STEAMED CAULIFLOWER WITH MUSTARD SAUCE

Serves: 4-6

This is a colorful and tasty way to dress up a winter vegetable.

1 head fresh young cauliflower, medium size
$\frac{1}{2}$ cup mayonnaise
1 tablespoon prepared mustard
1 tablespoon finely chopped parsley
Paprika

1. Cut cauliflower into approximate servings (4 to 6) and slash stems deeply.
2. Using vegetable steamer, place over boiling water. Cover and steam until done, 5 to 10 minutes.
3. Mix mayonnaise and mustard.
4. Top each serving with a portion of sauce. Sprinkle half of each serving with chopped parsley; the other half with paprika.

SLIM JIM CARROTS

These contain only a few calories but have lots of flavor.

> **1 pound carrots, peeled**
> **³/₄ teaspoon salt**
> **¹/₂ teaspoon sugar**
> **1 clove garlic, sliced**
> **¹/₂ medium onion, chopped**
> **1 teaspoon dill weed**
> **Dash of Cayenne pepper**
> **1 cup boiling water**
> **1 cup white wine vinegar**
> **Finely chopped parsley**

1. Cut carrots into sticks about 3 inches long by ¹/₄ inch wide; place in quart jar.
2. Add salt, sugar, garlic, onion, dill weed, and Cayenne.
3. Boil water and vinegar together; pour over carrots. Cool, cover tightly, and let stand 24 hours in refrigerator.
4. Lift from jar with tongs to serve. Garnish with freshly chopped parsley.

COINTREAU CARROTS

12 medium carrots
$1/2$ teaspoon salt
$1/2$ teaspoon sugar
1 cup water
1 large orange
1 tablespoon butter
$1/2$ cup Cointreau
$1/2$ teaspoon cornstarch

1. Peel, slice, and cook carrots with salt, sugar, and water until crisp-tender.

2. Peel orange with sharp paring knife, cutting off all white pith. Section orange and cut into bite-size pieces, retaining as much of the juice as possible.

3. When carrots are ready, pour off water; add butter, orange juice, and cornstarch which has been mixed with the Cointreau.

4. Cook until Cointreau thickens and the liquid is clear. Fold in orange pieces and serve.

All Italian cooks have a way with asparagus. One favorite is so simple but so delicious: hot asparagus topped with butter and grated Parmesan.

CELERY PARMESAN

Serves: 6
Temperature: 325°
Baking time: 20 minutes
9 x 5 x 2 inch pan

4 celery hearts, quartered
2 cups chicken broth
2 teaspoons chopped parsley
¹/₈ teaspoon minced garlic
¹/₂ cup grated Parmesan cheese
¹/₂ cup heavy cream
3 tablespoons butter, melted
¹/₂ teaspoon salt

1. Wash celery well.
2. In a large skillet, bring broth to boiling point.
3. Mix in parsley and garlic.
4. Add celery hearts in single layer.
5. Cover and simmer 15 minutes or until almost tender.
6. Drain and place in a buttered 9 x 5 x 2 inch baking dish.
7. Sprinkle with cheese.
8. Combine cream, butter, and salt and pour over celery.
9. Bake uncovered in a preheated 325° oven for 20 minutes or until celery is tender.

BURGUNDY ONIONS

Serves: 6-8

This dish is delicious with barbecued meats or wild game.

> **5 or 6 large sweet onions**
> **3 tablespoons butter**
> **4 to 5 whole cloves**
> **$\frac{1}{2}$ teaspoon salt**
> **1 cup Burgundy wine or other dry red wine**
> **1 cup pecans**
> **1 tablespoon butter**

1. Cut onions crosswise into $\frac{1}{4}$ inch slices; separate into rings. The ends may be held back and used in other dishes.

2. Heat butter in large, deep skillet or Dutch oven; add onion rings, tossing with a wooden spoon until thoroughly coated with butter.

3. Stir in cloves and salt and continue cooking until onions just start to brown.

4. Add wine, cover pan, and simmer about 15 minutes. Remove lid and cook on medium-high heat, stirring frequently, until wine is reduced to a glaze.

5. Sauté pecans in the 1 tablespoon butter in a separate skillet, then toss with glazed onion. Serve at once.

ZUCCHINI AU GRATIN

Serves: 8-10
Temperature: 375°
Baking time: 30-35 minutes
1¹/₂ quart shallow baking dish

8 medium (2 pounds) zucchini
¹/₄ cup minced onion
¹/₄ cup butter
2¹/₂ tablespoons flour
1 teaspoon salt
¹/₈ teaspoon nutmeg
Pinch each of cayenne and white peppers
1¹/₂ cups milk
2 tablespoons grated Parmesan cheese
1 cup shredded Swiss or Gruyère cheese

1. Place whole zucchini in large saucepan with boiling salted water to cover. Cook, covered, 7 to 8 minutes. Drain.

2. Cover zucchini with cold water. When cool, drain, then cut crosswise into ¹/₄ inch slices. Drain on towel.

3. Sauté onion in butter in large saucepan over medium heat until soft. Stir in flour, salt, nutmeg, cayenne, and white pepper. Cook, stirring constantly, until bubbly. Add milk gradually, stirring until thickened.

4. Remove from heat. Stir in Parmesan cheese and lightly fold in zucchini.

5. Spread mixture in buttered 1¹/₂ quart shallow baking dish. Sprinkle with Swiss or Gruyère cheese.

6. Bake in 375° oven until top is brown and bubbly, about 30 to 35 minutes. Garnish with paprika before serving.

Zucchini, a Quickie Vegetable

Cut off blossom ends of well-washed zucchini, one per person. Hold by stem and rub over medium grater to turn it into long shreds. Rub a green pepper over the same grater, figuring on 1 tablespoon per zucchini. Do the same with a halved onion. Toss together in a saucepan, add 1 or 2 tablespoons of butter and the same of water. Cover and cook over moderate heat 2 to 4 minutes, depending on the number of squash. This is a beautiful green with a crisp bite to it.

ZUCCHINI CHAOS

Serves: 4

1 tablespoon bacon drippings
1 tablespoon olive oil
4 medium-size zucchini, sliced thin
2 medium-size onions, sliced thin
Garlic salt to taste
Fresh ground pepper
Pinch of sugar
1 teaspoon dried oregano
1 tablespoon dry red table wine
1 tablespoon tomato paste
1 tablespoon grated Parmesan cheese
4 drops hot pepper sauce

1. In heavy skillet or electric frying pan, over medium heat, warm bacon drippings and olive oil. Add zucchini and onions; toss to coat.

2. Sprinkle with garlic salt and fresh ground pepper. Stir; add sugar and oregano.

3. Combine wine, tomato paste, Parmesan cheese, and hot pepper sauce. Add when zucchini starts to become transparent.

4. Serve when all is warm and mixed, but squash is still firm and somewhat crisp.

Dice 3 zucchini, cook until barely tender, put in shallow baking dish. Cover with a mixture of ½ cup sour cream, 2 tablespoons mayonnaise, 1 tablespoon lemon juice, salt, and pepper. Sprinkle with buttered crumbs; broil until bubbly. Double to serve six.

©Steve Crouch

Desserts

The desserts at Steinbeck House are so delicious and so popular that some people determine their luncheon reservation date according to the dessert offered. Imaginative Valley Guild cooks present here recipes for elegant desserts that are certain to provide a dramatic luncheon finale.

APPLE KUCHEN

Serves: 8
Temperature: 375°
Baking time: 35-40 minutes
11 to 12 inch flan with removable
bottom

PASTRY
1½ cups all-purpose flour
1 tablespoon sugar
¼ pound (1 stick) cold butter
Dash of salt
1 egg yolk, lightly beaten

1. Mix flour, sugar, butter and salt until fine as meal.

2. Stir in lightly beaten egg yolk.

3. Press into flan pan.

PASTRY TOPPING
4 tablespoons fine bread crumbs
2 teaspoons sugar
½ teaspoon cinnamon

1. Combine crumbs, sugar, and cinnamon thoroughly.

2. Sprinkle over the pastry.

FILLING
6 to 8 medium size pippin apples, peeled,
cored, and cut into very thin slices
6 tablespoons (¾ stick) butter, melted
and cooled
3 egg yolks, lightly beaten
6 tablespoons heavy cream

1. Overlap thin apple slices in a single layer around flan, completely covering the bottom.

2. Combine melted butter with beaten eggs. Add cream.

3. Pour over apples and bake until fork tender at 375° for 35-40 minutes.

4. After tart is baked, cover top with glaze (see below).

GLAZE
1 jar (10 ounces) currant jelly, melted

CINNAMON PUMPKIN FLAN

Serves: 6-8
Temperature: 350°
Baking time: 1 hour
9 inch glass pie plate

1¼ cups sugar
½ teaspoon salt
1 teaspoon cinnamon
1 cup pumpkin
5 large eggs, slightly beaten
2 cups light cream
½ pint whipping cream
¼ teaspoon ginger
2 teaspoons powdered sugar

1. Melt ½ cup of the sugar in bottom of 9 inch heat-proof glass pie plate over very low heat, stirring constantly until a golden syrup forms. Remove from heat and tip the plate back and forth until the sides and bottom are covered with caramel. Cool while you make the filling.

2. Combine the ¾ cup of sugar with the salt and cinnamon. Add pumpkin, eggs, and light cream. Mix well and pour into the caramel-coated pie plate. Set plate in a larger pan; pour in hot water until it comes about ½ inch up the outside of plate.

3. Bake 1 hour at 350°, or until a knife comes out clean. Chill.

4. When ready to serve, unmold upside-down onto a dish with a slight rim so none of the caramel will spill over the sides.

5. Garnish with the following topping: Combine whipping cream, ginger, and sugar. Whip to desired consistency.

CHOCOLATE SWIRL PECAN PIE

Serves: 8-10
Baking time: 15 minutes at 400°
40 minutes at 350°
9 inch pie pan

2 squares (2 ounces) unsweetened chocolate
1 tablespoon butter
½ cup granulated sugar
⅔ cup (1 small can) evaporated milk
1½ cups broken pecan pieces
1 tablespoon flour
3 eggs
1 cup light corn syrup
½ cup granulated sugar
¼ teaspoon salt
¼ teaspoon nutmeg
½ teaspoon cinnamon
1 teaspoon vanilla
2 tablespoons melted butter
9 inch unbaked pie shell

1. Melt chocolate in top of double boiler over very hot, not boiling, water.

2. Add butter and stir until melted.

3. Stirring constantly, add sugar; then slowly add evaporated milk, stirring until thick.

4. Remove from heat and let cool.

5. Stir together pecan pieces and flour. Set aside.

6. In large bowl beat eggs and beat in corn syrup, the other ½ cup sugar, salt, nutmeg, cinnamon, vanilla, and melted butter.

7. Fold in pecan-flour mixture.

8. Remove 1 cup of pecan mixture, then pour remainder into 9 inch unbaked pie shell.

9. Spoon chocolate-milk mixture in dollops over top of pie, swirling it into the filling with a knife to give a slight marbled effect.

10. Pour retained pecan mixture over chocolate.

11. Bake at 400° on middle rack of oven for 15 minutes; reduce heat to 350° and bake 40 minutes longer, or until knife inserted in center comes out clean.

12. Cool before serving.

*CHOCOLATE MALLOW PIE

Serves: 6-8
Temperature: 350°
Baking time: 8-10 minutes
9 inch pie pan

CRUST
¼ cup (½ stick) butter
1 cup graham cracker crumbs
¼ cup sugar
½ cup finely chopped nuts

1. Melt butter and combine with crumbs, sugar, and nuts. Press into 9 inch pie pan.
2. Bake 8 to 10 minutes in 350° oven, or until lightly browned. Cool.

FILLING
2 squares (2 ounces) unsweetened chocolate
½ pound miniature marshmallows
⅛ teaspoon salt
2 tablespoons water
2 eggs, separated
½ teaspoon vanilla
½ cup whipping cream
Whipping cream for garnish, if desired

1. In top of double boiler, melt the chocolate, marshmallows, salt, and water.
2. Beat egg yolks slightly and stir a little of the melted chocolate mixture into them; then stir the yolk mixture into the chocolate. Cook and stir over hot water about 2 minutes.
3. Remove from heat, add vanilla and cool.
4. Beat the ½ cup whipping cream stiff and fold into chocolate mixture.
5. Beat egg whites until stiff, but not dry, and fold into chocolate mixture.
6. Spoon into graham cracker crust and refrigerate. (Can be frozen.)
7. Garnish with additional whipped cream if desired.

*MALT SHOP PIE WITH CHOCOLATE CRUST

Serves: 6-8
9 inch pie pan

CRUST
2 cups crushed chocolate wafers
$\frac{1}{3}$ cup melted butter

1. Mix crumbs and butter together.
2. Press onto bottom and sides of the pie pan. Chill.

FILLING
1 pint vanilla ice cream
$\frac{1}{2}$ cup crushed malted milk balls
1 tablespoon milk
1 cup whipping cream
3 tablespoons chocolate-flavored malted milk powder
3 tablespoons marshmallow topping

1. Stir the ice cream to soften slightly.
2. Add milk and crushed malt balls.
3. Spread in cookie crust. Freeze.
4. Whip cream until soft peaks form.
5. Add malted milk powder and marshmallow topping to whipped cream.
6. Spread whipped cream mixture over ice cream layer.
7. Sprinkle pie with additional crushed malted milk balls or malted milk powder. Freeze.

BROWNIE PIE

Serves: 8-10
Temperature: 350°
Baking time: 30-40 minutes
9 inch pie pan

This dessert is very rich. Does not need refrigeration.

1 9 inch unbaked pie shell
1$\frac{1}{4}$ cups semi-sweet chocolate chips
$\frac{1}{2}$ cup (1 stick) butter
2 eggs
1 cup sugar
$\frac{1}{2}$ cup flour
1$\frac{1}{2}$ teaspoons vanilla
1$\frac{1}{4}$ cups pecans or walnuts, chopped fine
$\frac{1}{2}$ pint heavy cream, whipped, or
    vanilla ice cream

1. Prepare pie shell

2. Melt chocolate chips and set aside for marbling batter later.

3. Melt butter.

4. In large bowl, beat eggs with a wire whip.

5. Slowly add sugar, melted butter, flour, and vanilla. Beat well by hand.

6. Stir in nuts.

7. Slowly add melted chocolate and swirl through batter, not blending completely. The batter should look marbled.

8. Pour batter into unbaked pie shell and bake on middle rack of oven at 350° for 30 to 40 minutes, or until knife inserted in center comes out clean. Cool on rack.

9. If desired, serve with dollops of whipped cream or a la mode, with vanilla ice cream.

CHOCOLATE LOVER'S PIE

Serves: 8
Temperature: 250°
Baking time: 90 minutes
9 inch pie pan

If you like chocolate, you will love this rich and creamy filling in a meringue shell. Both the meringue and the filling must be prepared very early in the day or, better yet, the night before serving. Please use a good quality chocolate.

MERINGUE
4 large egg whites, brought to room
  temperature
¹/₄ teaspoon cream of tartar
1 cup granulated sugar
¹/₃ cup chopped pecans or walnuts

1. Generously butter the sides and bottom of a 9 inch pie pan.

2. Beat the egg whites and cream of tartar together at medium speed until frothy.

3. Sprinkle the sugar into the egg whites, a tablespoon at a time, as you continue beating. This should take 5 minutes. After all of the sugar has been added, continue to beat for 6 to 10 minutes. The sugar should be completely dissolved and the meringue should be very stiff and glossy. (To test, rub a bit of the meringue between the fingertips; it should feel very smooth.)

4. Spread the meringue over the bottom and sides of the pie pan to make a shell. Do not spread over the edge of the pan as it may make it difficult to remove.

5. Sprinkle the nuts over the bottom of the meringue.

6. Bake in a very slow oven, 250,° for 1¹/₂ hours. The meringue should turn to a pale gold color.

7. Cool on a rack out of a draft. Meringue may crack as it cools.

    NOTE: Frozen egg whites may be used successfully. Bring to room temperature before beating. Individual meringues may be made in different sizes and shapes by piping meringue through a pastry bag onto a cookie sheet covered with parchment paper.

Continued...

CHOCOLATE FILLING
4 ounces semi-sweet chocolate
2 ounces (2 squares) bittersweet chocolate
3 tablespoons strong coffee
1 teaspoon vanilla
1 cup whipping cream

1. Melt chocolate together over hot, not boiling, water. Stir in coffee. Heat and stir mixture until it is thick and smooth.
2. Remove from heat. Add vanilla. Cool.
3. Whip cream and fold into cooled chocolate mixture until well mixed.
4. Turn filling into the cooled meringue shell. Chill overnight.

TOPPING
1 cup whipping cream
2 tablespoons sifted powdered sugar
$\frac{1}{2}$ teaspoon vanilla

1. Whip cream, sugar, and vanilla until stiff enough to hold a shape.
2. Spread cream over pie, spoon in dollops, or squeeze through a pastry tube.

*CHOCOLATE CHEESE PIE IN COCOA CRUST

Serves: 8
Temperature: 375°
Baking time: 4 minutes
9 inch pie pan

CRUST
1 cup graham cracker crumbs
3 tablespoons unsweetened cocoa
2 tablespoons sugar
¼ cup sweet butter, melted

1. Combine crumbs, cocoa, sugar, and melted butter and press into bottom and sides of 9 inch pie pan.
2. Bake at 375° for 4 minutes. Cool.

FILLING
1 small package (6 ounces) semisweet chocolate chips
1 large package (8 ounces) cream cheese
½ cup brown sugar, packed
⅛ teaspoon salt
1 teaspoon vanilla
2 large eggs, separated
1 cup (½ pint) whipping cream
¼ cup (4 tablespoons) brown sugar
Extra whipped cream for topping

1. Melt chocolate chips in double boiler over hot, not boiling water. Remove from water and let cool.
2. Blend together the cream cheese, the ½ cup brown sugar, salt, and vanilla.
3. Beat in egg yolks and cooled chocolate.
4. Whip cream until stiff peaks form. Fold into chocolate mixture.
5. Beat egg whites with the ¼ cup brown sugar until stiff. Fold into above mixture.
6. Chill overnight.
7. To serve, top with whipped cream.

*LUSCIOUS ICE CREAM PIE WITH CHOCOLATE CRUST

Serves: 8
9 inch pie pan

CRUST
2 cups crushed chocolate wafers
$\frac{1}{3}$ cup melted butter

1. Mix crumbs and butter together.
2. Press into bottom and sides of 9 inch pie pan. Chill.

SAUCE
2 squares (2 ounces) unsweetened chocolate
$\frac{1}{2}$ cup sugar
1 tablespoon butter
$\frac{2}{3}$ cup (1 small can) evaporated milk

1. Melt chocolate over hot water. Stir in sugar and butter.
2. Slowly add evaporated milk.
3. Cook over hot water, stirring occasionally, until thickened. (It may take as long as 30 minutes). Chill.

FILLING
1 quart coffee ice cream, softened
1 cup whipping cream
1 ounce (2 tablespoons) white creme de cacao
$\frac{1}{2}$ cup chopped walnuts

1. Spread softened coffee ice cream over chocolate wafer crust. Put in freezer until ice cream is quite firm.
2. Spread chocolate sauce over ice cream.
3. Whip cream until stiff peaks form; add creme de cacao and mix. Spread over chocolate sauce.
4. Sprinkle chopped walnuts over top. Refreeze.

CHOCOLATE COCONUT BAVARIAN PIE

Serves: 8
9 inch pie pan

The rich chocolate crust has equal billing with the filling.

CRUST
2 squares (2 ounces) unsweetened chocolate
2 tablespoons butter
²/₃ cup sifted confectioners sugar
2 tablespoons hot milk
1¹/₂ cups snipped shredded coconut

1. Butter 9 inch pie pan.

2. In double boiler, melt chocolate squares and butter. Stir to blend.

3. Combine confectioners sugar and hot milk; stir into chocolate mixture. Add coconut and mix well.

4. Press into bottom and sides of pie pan. Refrigerate.

Continued...

COCONUT FILLING
1 envelope (1 tablespoon) unflavored gelatin
$\frac{1}{4}$ cup granulated sugar
3 eggs, separated
$1\frac{1}{4}$ cups milk
$\frac{1}{4}$ teaspoon salt
$\frac{1}{4}$ cup granulated sugar
1 cup whipping cream
$1\frac{1}{2}$ teaspoons vanilla
1 cup shredded coconut
1 square (1 ounce) unsweetened chocolate,
    grated

1. Combine gelatin with the $\frac{1}{4}$ cup sugar.

2. In double boiler top, beat egg yolks; stir in gelatin-sugar mixture and milk.

3. Cook over hot, not boiling, water, stirring until custard coats spoon (10 to 15 minutes).

4. Refrigerate, stirring occasionally, until custard mounds when dropped from spoon.

5. Beat egg whites until stiff. Add salt and the other $\frac{1}{4}$ cup sugar and keep beating until stiff peaks form.

6. Slowly stir in cool custard.

7. Whip cream until stiff, with vanilla, and slowly fold into custard mixture.

8. Stir in $\frac{1}{2}$ cup of coconut and pour into chocolate crust. Refrigerate.

9. Garnish top with the other $\frac{1}{2}$ cup coconut mixed with the grated unsweetened chocolate.

   To serve: Let stand at room temperature about 15 minutes before cutting.

Halve some smallish pears and put in baking dish. Spoon honey over, sprinkle with cinnamon, and pour in $\frac{1}{2}$ inch of muscatel or Madeira wine. Cover generously with macaroon crumbs. Cover and bake for $\frac{1}{2}$ hour in a moderate oven. Serve warm with whipped cream or sour cream.

*FRENCH MOCHA PIE

Serves: 8
Temperature: 300°
Baking time: 45 minutes
9 inch pie pan

1 cup sugar
1 teaspoon instant coffee powder
2 teaspoons cocoa
4 egg whites
$\frac{1}{2}$ teaspoon cream of tartar
$\frac{1}{2}$ cup crushed Ritz crackers (about 12)
$\frac{2}{3}$ cup finely chopped walnuts

1. Mix together sugar, coffee powder, and cocoa; set aside.
2. Using an electric mixer or rotary beater, beat egg whites and cream of tartar until soft peaks form.
3. Continue beating, adding the sugar-coffee mixture a little at a time until meringue is stiff and glossy.
4. Fold in cracker crumbs and nuts.
5. Turn into a lightly buttered and floured 9 inch pie pan, shaping mixture so it resembles a pie shell.
6. Bake at 300° for 45 minutes, or until meringue is firm. Cool.

TOPPING
1 tablespoon sugar
$\frac{1}{3}$ teaspoon instant coffee powder
$\frac{2}{3}$ teaspoon cocoa
1 cup ($\frac{1}{2}$ pint) whipping cream
Shaved chocolate

1. Mix sugar, coffee powder, and cocoa together.
2. Whip cream until soft peaks form.
3. Gradually add sugar mixture to cream and continue beating until cream is stiff.
4. No more than 1 hour before serving, spread topping over pie and garnish with a sprinkling of shaved chocolate.

*RODEO PIE WITH VANILLA CRUMB CRUST

Serves: 8
Freezing time: 2 hours or more
9 inch pie pan

CRUST
1¹/₂ cups crushed vanilla wafers (about 36)
¹/₃ cup melted butter

1. Mix together crushed vanilla wafers and melted butter.
2. Press into sides and bottom of a buttered 9 inch pie pan.
3. Freeze.

FILLING
1 cup sugar
1 tablespoon light corn syrup
¹/₈ teaspoon salt
³/₄ cup milk
2 tablespoons butter
¹/₃ cup creamy peanut butter
¹/₂ teaspoon vanilla
1¹/₂ bananas, sliced
1 quart vanilla ice cream
1 cup whipping cream
¹/₄ cup chopped peanuts

1. In saucepan, mix together sugar, corn syrup, salt, and milk. Stir over moderate heat until boiling. Boil slowly about 10 minutes. (Sauce will <u>not</u> be thick.)
2. Remove from heat and add, stirring briskly: butter, peanut butter, and vanilla. Cool.
3. Arrange banana slices in frozen crust. Cover with scoops of vanilla ice cream. (Use scoops so sauce will be able to run through the crevices.)
4. Pour or spread cooled sauce over ice cream. Freeze.
5. When ready to serve, whip cream and place a spoonful on each piece of pie. Sprinkle with the chopped peanuts.

   NOTE: You may have some sauce left over; refrigerate and use for sundaes.

*BRANDY ALEXANDER PIE

Serves: 6-8
Temperature: 350°
Baking time: 10 minutes
9 inch pie pan

Even if you don't like an Alexander, you'll like this flavor combination.

CRUST
1¹/₂ cups graham cracker crumbs
2 tablespoons sugar
6 tablespoons melted butter

1. Combine crumbs, sugar, and butter; press into pie pan.
2. Bake at 350° for 10 minutes. Cool.

FILLING
1 tablespoon (1 envelope) unflavored gelatin
¹/₂ cup cold water
²/₃ cup sugar
¹/₈ teaspoon salt
3 eggs, separated
¹/₄ cup Cognac (brandy)
¹/₄ cup Creme de Cacao
¹/₃ cup sugar
1 cup whipping cream
Garnish: whipped cream and chocolate curls

1. Soften gelatin in cold water in saucepan.
2. Add sugar, salt, and slightly beaten egg yolks to gelatin mixture. Over low heat, stir together until gelatin is dissolved and mixture thickens.
3. Remove from heat and stir in the Cognac and Creme de Cacao.
4. Chill in refrigerator until mixture mounds slightly and thickens.
5. Beat the 3 egg whites until frothy. Add the ¹/₃ cup sugar slowly and continue beating until stiff.
6. Beat cream until stiff.
7. Fold egg whites into gelatin mixture and then fold in the whipped cream.
8. Pile into graham cracker crust.
9. Chill several hours or overnight.
10. Garnish with whipped cream and semisweet chocolate curls.

SANTA ROSA PLUM CHIFFON PIE

A beautiful pie with a most delicate and unusual flavor.

1 9 inch baked pastry shell
2 cups sliced, very ripe Santa Rosa plums
    (The plums must be dark red and soft.)
1 tablespoon (1 envelope) unflavored gelatin
3 slightly beaten egg yolks
³/₄ cup sugar
¹/₂ teaspoon lemon juice
3 egg whites
1 cup heavy cream, whipped
2 or 3 unpeeled plums

1. Purée plums in blender or food processor to make 1 cup purée.

2. Pour purée into medium saucepan and sprinkle gelatin over top of purée. Add slightly beaten egg yolks, ¹/₂ cup of the sugar, and lemon juice. Mix well. Cook over low heat, stirring constantly, until gelatin dissolves and mixture thickens slightly.

3. Chill mixture, stirring occasionally, until mixture mounds slightly when dropped with a spoon.

4. Beat egg whites until soft peaks form, gradually adding the remaining ¹/₄ cup sugar. Continue to beat until stiff.

5. Whip cream.

6. Fold egg whites and whipped cream into plum mixture so it gives a marbled effect. Chill, if necessary, until filling will pile high. Turn into pastry shell and chill several hours or overnight.

7. Garnish with thin slices of unpeeled plums.

PASTRY CRUST

This recipe makes 3 double crusts.

**6 cups sifted flour
2 teaspoons salt
2¼ cups vegetable shortening
Ice water**

1. Mix together flour and salt; cut in shortening with a pastry blender until particles are the size of peas.
2. Gradually sprinkle ice water over mixture until flour is just moist and mixture forms a ball. Refrigerate for 20 to 30 minutes.
3. If making single crust, roll out to fit pie pan, crimp edges, and prick bottom and sides of shell with a fork. Bake at 450° for 10 minutes or until lightly browned.

*CRANBERRY RASPBERRY PIE

*Serves: 8
Temperature: 375°
Baking time: 30-35 minutes
9 inch pie pan
2 quart saucepan*

**1 package (10 ounces) frozen raspberries, thawed
3 cups (12 ounce package) fresh cranberries
1½ cups sugar
3 tablespoons cornstarch
¼ teaspoon salt
1 9 inch unbaked pastry crust**

1. Drain liquid from raspberries; add enough water to drained juice to make ½ cup liquid.
2. In saucepan bring to a boil the raspberry liquid and the fresh cranberries; simmer for about 15 minutes or until cranberries have popped.
3. Combine thoroughly the sugar, cornstarch, and salt; stir into hot cranberry mixture.
4. Cook quickly, stirring constantly, until mixture thickens and bubbles.
5. Remove from heat and stir in thawed raspberries.
6. Pour into unbaked pastry crust; bake in 375° oven for 30 to 35 minutes or until set.

*CRANBERRY PECAN PIE

Serves: 8
Temperature: 375°
Baking time: 1 hour
9 inch pie pan

The cranberries add excitement to a very rich pie filling.

3 eggs
²/₃ cup sugar
¹/₈ teaspoon salt
1 cup dark corn syrup
¹/₃ cup butter, melted
1 cup coarsely chopped cranberries
1 cup pecan halves, chopped
1 unbaked 9 inch pie crust

1. Beat eggs slightly. Add sugar and salt and mix until sugar dissolves.
2. Stir in corn syrup and melted butter and mix well. Stir in cranberries and pecans.
3. Pour into unbaked pie crust. To prevent over-browning, cover edge of pie with foil.
4. Bake at 375° for 1 hour or until done (when knife is inserted in center and comes out clean).
5. Cool thoroughly. Garnish with whipped cream.

Don't forget raspberries, boysenberries, olallieberries. All three have an affinity for coconut. For a switch though, stir coconut into slightly softened vanilla ice cream, and return to freezing compartment. Serve sweetened berries over scoops of the coconut cream.

GLAZED FRUIT PIE

Serves: 6-8
9 inch pie pan

If olallieberries are not available, use any fresh fruit such as strawberries, peaches, or black raspberries. All make a delicious picture pie.

1 9 inch baked pie shell
4 cups fresh olallieberries, washed and
   drained
1 cup water
3 tablespoons cornstarch
1 cup sugar
1 teaspoon lemon juice
1 cup heavy cream, whipped
2 teaspoons powdered sugar
¹/₄ teaspoon vanilla

1. Fill baked pie shell with 3 cups of the washed and drained berries.

2. Combine remaining 1 cup berries with water in a saucepan. Cook over medium heat 3 or 4 minutes.

3. Combine cornstarch and sugar; add to cooking berries. Cook over medium heat, stirring constantly until mixture has thickened and becomes transparent. Add lemon juice. Force through a sieve or food mill. Cool slightly.

4. Pour glaze over berries in pastry shell. Chill thoroughly for 2 or 3 hours.

5. Whip cream to soft peaks. Add powdered sugar and vanilla. Continue to whip until the mixture stands in stiff peaks. Decorate the pie.

   NOTE: This pie does not hold well. On the second day, or if it stands overnight, the glaze separates from fruit.

188

CREAMY BERRY PIE WITH GINGER CRUST

Serves: 8
9 inch pie pan

CRUST
$\frac{1}{4}$ cup ($\frac{1}{2}$ stick) butter, melted
$1\frac{1}{4}$ cups fine ginger-snap crumbs

1. Combine butter and crumbs in a small bowl; blend with a fork or fingers.
2. Press evenly on bottom and sides of pie pan. Chill until ready to fill.

FILLING
$\frac{1}{2}$ cup (1 stick) butter
$2\frac{1}{2}$ cups sifted powdered sugar
2 eggs
$\frac{1}{2}$ cup fine ginger-snap crumbs
1 cup whipping cream
$\frac{1}{4}$ cup sugar
2 cups fresh olallieberries
$\frac{3}{4}$ cup chopped pecans
A few whole berries for garnish

1. Cream butter and gradually add sugar.
2. Beat in eggs, one at a time.
3. Spread this mixture in crumb crust.
4. Sprinkle the $\frac{1}{2}$ cup ginger-snap crumbs evenly over butter-egg layer.
5. Whip cream and sugar together. Fold in berries and pecans. Spoon this mixture over ginger-snap crumbs.
6. Chill at least 2 hours, and until serving time.
7. Cut in wedges and garnish with fresh berries.

   NOTE: Raspberries, boysenberries, strawberries, or fresh peaches may be substituted for olallieberries.

*PUMPKIN PRALINE PIE

Serves: 6-8

1 baked 9 inch pie shell
⅓ cup butter
⅓ cup brown sugar, packed
½ cup chopped pecans
3 eggs, separated
⅔ cup milk
½ cup sugar
1¼ cups canned pumpkin
½ teaspoon each cinnamon, ginger,
   and nutmeg
¼ teaspoon each pumpkin pie spice
   and salt
1 envelope (1 tablespoon) unflavored gelatin
¼ cup cold water
6 tablespoons sugar

1. In small skillet, combine butter and brown sugar. Cook over medium heat, stirring constantly, until mixture bubbles vigorously. Remove from stove. Add pecans, stirring until mixture is crumbly. Set aside to cool.

2. In top of double boiler, beat egg yolks slightly, add milk, the ½ cup sugar, pumpkin, salt, and spices. Cook over hot water, stirring constantly, until thickened to custard consistency.

3. Soften gelatin in cold water. Dissolve in hot custard. Cool until slightly thickened.

4. Beat egg whites until quite frothy. Add the 6 tablespoons sugar, one at a time. Continue beating until heavy, soft peaks form.

5. Fold egg white into pumpkin mixture until blended.

6. Sprinkle pecan mixture over baked pie shell, reserving 3 tablespoons for top of pie.

7. Pour pumpkin filling into prepared shell and chill for several hours.

8. Just before serving, sprinkle remaining pecan mixture over top of pie. Garnish each serving with whipped cream, if desired.

*SOUR CREAM PUMPKIN PIE

Serves: 8
Temperature: 375°
Baking time: 5 minutes
9 inch pie pan

3/4 cup light brown sugar, packed
1 envelope (1 tablespoon) unflavored gelatin
1 teaspoon cinnamon
1/2 teaspoon cloves
1/2 teaspoon nutmeg
1/2 teaspoon salt
3 eggs, separated
1/2 cup milk
1 can (16 ounces) pumpkin
1 cup (1/2 pint) sour cream
1/4 cup granulated sugar
Ginger-snap crust (see below) or baked
  pastry shell

1. In a large saucepan, combine brown sugar, gelatin, cinnamon, cloves, nutmeg, and salt.
2. In a large mixing bowl, beat the 3 egg yolks slightly, add milk and canned pumpkin, and blend well.
3. Add egg yolk mixture to ingredients in saucepan. Mix well and cook over medium heat, stirring constantly, until slightly thickened and gelatin is dissolved. Remove from heat.
4. Cool slightly, then add sour cream.
5. Refrigerate until mixture forms soft mounds.
6. In a mixer bowl, beat the egg whites until foamy and then gradually add the 1/4 cup sugar. Continue beating until stiff but not dry.
7. Fold egg whites into cooled pumpkin mixture.
8. Pour into prepared pie shell and chill for at least 4 hours or overnight.
9. Garnish with whipped cream.

GINGER-SNAP CRUST
1 1/2 cups fine ginger-snap crumbs
1/4 cup melted butter

1. Combine crumbs and melted butter. Mix well and press into sides and bottom of 9 inch pie pan.
2. Bake at 375° for 5 minutes. Cool.

*PUMPKIN MALLOW PIE WITH GINGER-SNAP CRUST

Serves: 6-8
Temperature: 350°
Baking time: 5 minutes
9 inch pie pan

The ginger in the crust adds extra zing to the filling.

CRUST
1¹/₃ cups crushed ginger-snaps
¹/₄ cup sugar
¹/₄ cup soft butter

1. Mix crushed ginger-snaps, sugar, and butter together. Press into bottom and sides of 9 inch pie pan.
2. Bake at 350° for 5 minutes or until lightly browned. Cool.

FILLING
1 can (16 ounces) pumpkin
1 bag (10 ounces) small marshmallows
1 teaspoon cinnamon
¹/₂ teaspoon ginger
¹/₂ teaspoon salt
2 cups heavy cream
2 tablespoons sugar

1. Combine pumpkin, marshmallows, cinnamon, ginger, and salt and heat over boiling water, stirring occasionally, until marshmallows are melted. Mix well. Cool at room temperature.
2. Whip together the heavy cream and sugar. Fold into cooled pumpkin mixture. Pour into baked ginger-snap pie shell.
3. Refrigerate until serving time.
4. Each serving may be topped with a whipped cream flower before serving.

*LEMON SURPRISE

Serves: 6-8
Temperature: 350°
Baking time: 10-15 minutes
9 inch pie pan

CRUST
¹/₂ cup (1 stick) butter
1 cup flour
¹/₂ cup finely chopped walnuts

1. Cut butter into flour until like cornmeal.
2. Mix in walnuts. Reserve ³/₄ cup. Press remainder into bottom and sides of 9 inch pie pan.
3. Bake at 350° for 10 to 15 minutes or until lightly browned. Cool.

FILLING
4 egg yolks
¹/₂ cup sugar
3 tablespoons lemon juice
1 tablespoon finely grated lemon peel
¹/₄ teaspoon salt (optional)
1 cup powdered sugar
1 large package (8 ounces) cream cheese
¹/₂ cup whipping cream

1. In top of double boiler, mix together egg yolks, sugar, lemon juice, lemon peel, and salt.
2. Cook over hot, not boiling, water until thickened, stirring with whisk. Cool.
3. Beat powdered sugar and cream cheese together until fluffy.
4. Whip cream until soft peaks form.
5. Fold whipped cream into cream-cheese mixture; add cooled lemon mixture. Pour into cooled pie shell.
6. Garnish with reserved ³/₄ cup crumbs.
7. Refrigerate.

*PECAN CRUNCH PIE

Serves: 6-8
Temperature: 350°
Baking time: 25 minutes
9 inch pie pan

This dessert is delicious when served chilled but is especially delightful while still warm.

3 eggs
¹/₂ teaspoon baking powder
1 cup sugar
1 cup graham cracker crumbs
1 cup chopped pecans
1 teaspoon vanilla

TOPPING
1 cup whipping cream
2 tablespoons sugar
1 teaspoon vanilla

1. Beat together the eggs and baking powder.
2. Slowly add the sugar and continue beating until very thick.
3. Mix together the graham cracker crumbs and pecans; fold into the egg mixture. Add vanilla and blend.
4. Spread the mixture in a heavily buttered 9 inch pie pan and bake for 25 minutes at 350.°
5. Beat the whipping cream with the 2 tablespoons sugar and the other teaspoon of vanilla until stiff.
6. Cut dessert in wedges and serve with a dollop of whipped cream topping.

To toast walnut meats, drop in rapidly boiling water and boil 3 minutes. Drain well, then spread evenly in shallow pan and bake in moderate oven for 15 to 20 minutes, stirring often. When treated this way they won't lose their crispness in a salad or a dessert.

*ICE CREAM CAKE WITH GINGER-SNAP CRUST

Serves: 12
9 inch springform pan

**1¹/₂ cups ginger-snap crumbs
(about 24 snaps)
¹/₃ cup butter, melted**

1. In a medium bowl, mix ginger-snap crumbs and melted butter.
2. Press mixture to the bottom and sides of a 9 inch springform pan.
3. Bake crust 8 minutes in a 375° oven. Cool.

**FILLING
1 package (10 ounces) frozen raspberries
2 small cans (9 ounces each) crushed
    pineapple, drained
1 tablespoon lemon juice concentrate
2 quarts vanilla ice cream, softened
1 can (6 ounces) frozen orange juice
    concentrate, thawed
1 teaspoon almond flavoring
1 teaspoon rum flavoring
Whipped cream and toasted sliced almonds**

1. Thaw raspberries and mash in blender.
2. Strain to remove seeds, then mix with drained, crushed pineapple, and lemon concentrate. Place mixture in freezer to partially freeze.
3. Mix 1 quart of the softened ice cream with the orange juice concentrate. Spoon this mixture into cooled ginger-snap crumb crust and put in freezer.
4. Beat partially frozen raspberry-pineapple mixture and pour over frozen ice cream layer. Freeze again.
5. Mix together remaining quart of softened vanilla ice cream and almond and rum flavorings; spoon on top of raspberry-pineapple layer. Freeze until firm.
6. Cut in wedges and garnish with whipped cream and toasted almonds.

CHOCOLATE MINT ROLL

Serves: 10
Temperature: 350°
Baking time: 12 minutes
15½ x 10½ inch pan

CAKE
6 egg whites
½ teaspoon cream of tartar
½ cup sugar
6 egg yolks
½ cup sugar
3 tablespoons flour
¼ teaspoon salt
¼ cup unsweetened cocoa
1 teaspoon vanilla

1. Beat egg whites and cream of tartar until foamy.
2. Gradually beat in the ½ cup sugar. Mixture should look glossy.
3. In separate bowl, beat egg yolks until thick and lemon-colored. Beat the other ½ cup sugar into egg yolks.
4. Sift together flour, salt, and cocoa; stir into yolk mixture along with vanilla.
5. Carefully fold egg white mixture into cake batter.
6. Spread mixture into shallow jelly-roll pan lined with well-greased wax paper.
7. Bake at 350° for 12 minutes or just until surface springs back when touched lightly with finger.
8. Immediately turn out of pan, upside down, onto dish towel sprinkled with powdered sugar.
9. Pull off wax paper at once. By lifting the end of towel, roll cake into a "log." Wrap in towel and cool. Add filling (see below).

FILLING
1 package (3 ounces) cream cheese
½ cup powdered sugar
1 cup whipping cream
1 tablespoon creme de menthe or ½
   teaspoon peppermint flavoring
Green food coloring
Powdered sugar trim

1. Beat cream cheese and powdered sugar together.
2. Whip cream; add creme de menthe.
3. Tint cream a pretty green color.
4. Carefully unroll cake and spread mint filling over top.
5. Roll cake again; chill until serving time.
6. Just before serving, sprinkle top of cake roll with powdered sugar.

DE LUXE
LEMON ROLL

Serves: 8
Temperature: 375°
Baking time: 15 minutes
15¹/₂ x 10¹/₂ x 1 inch jelly-roll pan

CAKE
³/₄ cup sifted cake flour
³/₄ teaspoon baking powder
¹/₄ teaspoon salt
4 large eggs
³/₄ cup sugar
1 teaspoon vanilla
Sifted confectioners sugar

1. Sift flour, baking powder, and salt. Set aside.

2. Beat eggs with electric mixer until light in color. Gradually add sugar, then vanilla. Beat at high speed for 5 minutes or until thick and a light lemon color.

3. Fold dry ingredients into egg mixture. Spread batter in wax-paper-lined jelly-roll pan.

4. Bake at 375° for 15 minutes, or until top springs back when lightly touched with finger.

5. Turn from pan onto a kitchen towel dusted with sifted confectioners sugar. Remove wax paper and cut off any crisp edges immediately. Roll up, starting at narrow end, rolling up towel with cake. Cool completely.

6. Unroll cake, remove towel, and spread with lemon filling (see below) to within ¹/₂ inch of edge. Reroll cake. Dust with more confectioners sugar. Chill until serving time.

LEMON FILLING
¹/₄ cup (¹/₂ stick) butter
1 cup sugar
3 large eggs, slightly beaten
Grated peel of 1 lemon
6 tablespoons strained lemon juice
¹/₈ teaspoon salt

1. Melt butter in heavy saucepan over low heat.

2. Combine sugar, slightly beaten eggs, lemon peel, lemon juice, and salt. Add to melted butter.

3. Cook over low heat, stirring constantly with a wooden spoon until well thickened. Cool and store covered. (This keeps well for several days.)

DOUBLE CHOCOLATE BROWNIES

Serves: 25 (cookies)
Temperature: 350°
Baking time: 30-35 minutes
9 inch square pan

A rich, moist brownie that can be served as a cookie or cut into larger pieces, then topped with a scoop of ice cream and chocolate sauce.

¹/₂ cup (1 stick) butter
2 squares (2 ounces) unsweetened chocolate
¹/₂ cup semi-sweet chocolate chips
2 large eggs
1 cup sugar
1 teaspoon vanilla
¹/₂ cup all-purpose flour
1 cup miniature marshmallows
¹/₂ cup chopped pecans

1. Melt butter, chocolate, and chocolate chips together in a heavy saucepan over low heat, or over hot, not boiling, water.

2. Beat eggs until thick and lemon-colored with a mixer. Add sugar gradually while continuing to beat. Add vanilla.

3. Gradually beat chocolate mixture into egg and sugar mixture.

4. Stir in flour, marshmallows, and chopped pecans.

5. Bake in greased 9 inch square pan at 350° for 30 to 35 minutes, or until a toothpick inserted in the middle comes out clean. Do not overbake.

6. Remove from oven and cool 15 minutes on a wire rack. While cake is still warm, cut into squares with a thin, sharp knife.

7. Store brownies in an airtight container with wax paper between layers.

COFFEE MERINGUE CAKE

Serves: 6

Parchment paper
5 extra-large egg whites, room temperature
$1/2$ teaspoon cream of tartar
$1/4$ teaspoon salt
$1^1/4$ cups superfine sugar*

1. Preheat oven to 450°

2. Cut parchment paper to fit large cookie sheet. Trace two 7 inch circles on paper with at least 1 inch separating the circles.

3. Beat egg whites until frothy; add cream of tartar and salt. Continue to beat until soft peaks form.

4. Gradually add sugar, beating until stiff and glossy.

5. Heap meringue equally on the two 7 inch circles drawn on parchment paper. Gently form meringue into layer-cake shape with spatula.

6. Place in preheated oven. *Close door immediately and turn off heat.* Leave oven door closed 8 hours or overnight. Do not peek.

FILLING
1 cup whipping cream
2 teaspoons instant coffee crystals
2 teaspoons superfine sugar*
1 square (1 ounce) semi-sweet chocolate, grated
1 tablespoon Kahlua (optional)

1. Whip cream; fold in coffee crystals and sugar.

2. Cover one meringue with half the cream mixture; sprinkle with grated chocolate. Place second layer of meringue on first layer and repeat. Chill thoroughly.

3. Pour the Kahlua liqueur carefully over the top, if desired. Cut as you would a layer cake.

*If superfine sugar not available, put sugar in blender a few seconds.

*FORGOTTEN LEMON TORTE

Serves: 12
Temperature: 450°
Baking time: 8 hours or overnight
—takes 2 days
9 inch springform pan

The egg whites make the meringue shell; the egg yolks thicken the lemon filling.

MERINGUE
5 extra-large egg whites, room temperature
½ teaspoon cream of tartar
¼ teaspoon salt
1¼ cups fine sugar (for extra-fine sugar,
    run in blender)

1. Preheat oven to 450.°
2. Beat egg whites until frothy; add cream of tartar and salt; continue to beat until soft peaks form.
3. Gradually add sugar, beating until stiff and glossy.
4. Turn into a buttered 9 inch springform pan. Spread evenly.
5. Place in pre-heated oven, *close door immediately and turn off heat.* Leave oven door closed 8 hours or overnight. *Do not peek.*

LEMON FILLING
5 egg yolks, slightly beaten
½ cup sugar
¼ cup lemon juice
1 tablespoon grated lemon peel
¼ teaspoon salt
1 cup whipping cream
1 cup whipping cream for garnishing

1. In the top of a double boiler, combine yolks, sugar, lemon juice, lemon peel, and salt.
2. Cook over hot water until thickened, stirring occasionally. Cool.
3. Whip cream.
4. To assemble: Spread half of the whipped cream over meringue, then half of the lemon filling over the cream. Repeat, spreading to edges. Cover with foil or plastic wrap. Chill 24 hours.
5. Remove ring and garnish with remaining whipped cream.

*PINEAPPLE BLITZ TORTE

Serves: 10
Temperature: 350°
Baking time: 30 minutes
2 8 inch cake pans

A pineapple filling adds distinction to the layers of meringue-topped cake.

1. First, make the meringue that bakes on the cake: beat 4 egg whites until foamy. Gradually add $3/4$ cup sugar, beating until moist peaks form.
2. Add 1 teaspoon vanilla. Set aside.

CAKE
$1/4$ cup ($1/2$ stick) butter
$1/2$ cup sugar
4 egg yolks, thoroughly beaten
1 cup cake flour
$1/4$ teaspoon salt
$2 1/2$ teaspoons baking powder
$1/3$ cup milk
$3/4$ cup chopped walnuts

1. Thoroughly cream butter and sugar.
2. Add egg yolks and beat well.
3. Sift together flour, salt, and baking powder.
4. Add dry ingredients to mixture alternately with the milk.
5. Line 8 inch cake pans with wax paper. Divide mixture between two pans.
6. Bake at 350° for 15 minutes.
7. Remove pans from oven and quickly spread meringue over tops of partially baked layers.
8. Sprinkle chopped walnuts over meringue and return pans to oven.
9. Bake at 350° for 15 minutes longer. Remove from oven and let stand on racks 15 minutes before removing from pans.
10. Let cool before filling.

PINEAPPLE FILLING
1 cup heavy cream
$1 1/2$ tablespoons powdered sugar
$1/4$ teaspoon vanilla
1 cup crushed pineapple, very well drained

1. Whip cream until stiff, gradually adding sugar and vanilla.
2. Fold in pineapple.
3. Place one layer of cake, meringue side <u>down</u>, on cake plate. Spread with filling.
4. Top with second cake layer, meringue side <u>up</u>.

*GRAHAM CRACKER TORTE WITH CARAMEL SAUCE

Serves: 16
Temperature: 325°
Baking time: 25 minutes
2 9 inch round cake pans

For best flavor, make this the day before serving and refrigerate.

6 eggs, separated
1¹/₂ cups sugar
1 teaspoon baking powder
1 teaspoon vanilla
1 teaspoon almond extract
¹/₂ teaspoon salt
2 cups graham cracker crumbs
1 cup finely chopped walnuts
2 cups (1 pint) whipping cream
Caramel sauce (see below)

1. Grease and flour two 9 inch round cake pans.
2. Beat egg yolks until thick and lemon-colored.
3. Gradually add sugar to yolks and beat until mixture forms ribbons, about 10 minutes.
4. Add baking powder, vanilla, and almond extract to egg yolks and mix well. Set aside.
5. Beat egg whites and salt until stiff but not dry.
6. Mix graham cracker crumbs and chopped nuts together.
7. Gently fold the egg yolk mixture and then the crumbs into the beaten egg whites.
8. Divide between the 2 prepared pans. Bake at 325° for 25 minutes. Cool, remove from pans, and assemble, preferably the day before serving.
9. While torte is baking, make the sauce and beat the cream.

CARAMEL SAUCE
1 egg
¹/₂ cup brown sugar, packed
2 tablespoons butter
2 tablespoons orange juice
2 tablespoons flour
¹/₂ teaspoon vanilla

1. Beat egg, sugar, butter, orange juice, and flour together. Cook over low heat until thickened. Add vanilla.
2. Cool at room temperature (not more than 2 hours).
3. To assemble cake: Spread half (1 cup) of the whipped cream between torte layers. Frost top with the rest of the whipped cream. Drizzle the caramel sauce over top, allowing some to run down sides. Decorate top with additional chopped walnuts.

*MOCHA NUT TORTE

Serves: 8
Temperature: 300°
Baking time: 40 minutes
2 9 inch round cake pans

A rich mocha filling slipcovers a nut-filled torte.

FILLING
¹/₂ cup sugar
¹/₈ teaspoon salt
1 ounce (1 square) unsweetened chocolate
1 cup strong liquid coffee
1 tablespoon butter
2 teaspoons vanilla
1 cup cream, whipped

1. In top of double boiler, mix together sugar, salt, chocolate, coffee, and butter. Cook over boiling water, stirring constantly, until thick and smooth.
2. Blend in vanilla. Cool thoroughly. Make the cake part while filling is cooling.
3. When cooled, fold in whipped cream.

TORTE
6 eggs, separated
³/₄ cup sugar
¹/₄ cup flour
¹/₄ cup sugar
1 cup walnuts, finely ground
¹/₂ cup finely ground dry bread crumbs

1. Beat egg yolks until thick. Slowly add the ³/₄ cup sugar and ¹/₄ cup flour and beat until very thick and pale.
2. Beat egg whites until foamy. Slowly add the ¹/₄ cup sugar and beat until soft peaks form.
3. Mix nuts and bread crumbs together.
4. Fold whites into yolks alternately with nut mixture.
5. Spoon into two 9 inch round cake pans which have had bottoms greased, then lined with wax paper that also has been greased.
6. Bake at 300° for 40 minutes or until only faint imprint remains when tops are touched. Let cool, then remove from pans and pull off wax paper.
7. When cold, frost middle, top, and sides with Mocha Nut Filling.

*ELEGANT CHOCOLATE CHEESECAKE WITH A CHOCOLATE CRUST

Serves: 12-16
Temperature: 350°
Baking time: 1 hour 20 minutes
9 inch springform pan

CRUST
2 cups chocolate wafer cookie crumbs
¼ cup sugar
¼ teaspoon cinnamon
7 tablespoons butter, melted

1. Blend cookie crumbs, sugar, and cinnamon with melted butter.

2. With a spoon, press crumbs over bottom and up 3 inches around side of a 9 inch cheesecake pan (with removable bottom or spring-release sides).

FILLING
4 eggs
1½ cups sugar
6 tablespoons cocoa
1 teaspoon vanilla
**2 packages (8 ounces each) cream cheese,
    room temperature**
4 cups (2 pints) sour cream

1. In a blender, combine eggs, sugar, cocoa, vanilla, and 1 of the 8 ounce packages of cream cheese. Cover and whirl until smooth; pour about half the mixture into a bowl. Put remaining cream cheese in blender, cover, and blend until smooth.

2. Stir sour cream into cheese-cocoa mixture in the bowl, then mix in remaining smooth cheese in blender. (If using a mixer, beat cheese until smooth, then mix in sugar, cocoa, vanilla, eggs — 1 at a time, and sour cream.)

3. Pour mixture into the chocolate crust.

4. Bake at 350° for 1 hour 20 minutes, or until edge is set and dull in color, while an area about 4 inches in diameter in center looks glossy. Cool; cover and chill thoroughly.

5. Remove pan rim and set cake on a serving dish. Pile the cream topping (see next page) in the center of the cake. Sprinkle with grated chocolate.

Continued...

TOPPING
1 package (3 ounces) cream cheese
$^1/_2$ cup whipping cream
$^1/_4$ cup powdered sugar
1 tablespoon creme de cacao or Kahlua
1 ounce semi-sweet chocolate

1. In a small bowl of electric mixer, blend the cream cheese until soft; gradually add whipping cream and mix at high speed until mixture is the consistency of stiffly whipped cream.

2. Blend in powdered sugar and creme de cacao or Kahlua. Cover and chill until ready to decorate cake.

3. Grate (or shave with a vegetable peeler) the semi-sweet chocolate. Sprinkle topping with grated chocolate.

Apple Cream

To each cup of applesauce add $^1/_2$ cup sour cream. Spoon into dishes and chill. Just before serving sprinkle each with about 2 tablespoons brown sugar and 1 to 2 tablespoons chopped nutmeats.

Another combination of mellow and crisp: combine seeded grapes (or seedless whole grapes) with brown sugar and just enough dairy sour cream to hold them together. A little vanilla does no harm because it brings out the flavor of the grapes and helps blend with other ingredients.

*PRALINE CHEESECAKE

Serves: 12-16
Temperature: 350°
Baking time: 1 hour 10 minutes
9 inch springform pan

This is a very rich and delicious dessert and can be prepared ahead of time. Garnish with additional chopped pecans if desired.

CRUST
1 cup graham cracker crumbs
3 tablespoons sugar
3 tablespoons melted butter

1. Combine crumbs, sugar, and butter. Press onto bottom of springform pan.
2. Bake for 10 minutes at 350.°

FILLING
3 large packages (8 ounces each) cream cheese, softened
1½ cups dark brown sugar, packed
4 eggs
2 cups sour cream
1½ teaspoons vanilla
½ cup finely chopped pecans

1. In mixer, blend together the softened cream cheese and brown sugar.
2. Add eggs, one at a time, beating well with each addition.
3. Blend in the sour cream, vanilla, and pecans.
4. Pour over crust. Bake for 1 hour and 10 minutes at 350.° When done, the center will appear to be a little soft and shiny. Cool in pan on wire rack.

TOPPING
1 small package (3 ounces) cream cheese, softened
½ cup dark brown sugar, packed
1 cup heavy cream, whipped

1. Cream together the softened cream cheese and brown sugar until smooth.
2. Fold in the whipped cream; spread mixture over the top of cooled cake. Chill thoroughly.
3. Remove sides of pan.

*RASPBERRY CHEESECAKE

Serves: 12-16
Temperature: 350°
Baking time: 50-55 minutes
9 inch springform pan

CRUST
1¼ cups graham cracker crumbs
2 tablespoons sugar
2 tablespoons butter, melted

1. Mix cracker crumbs, sugar, and melted butter together and press into 9 inch springform pan.
2. Bake for 10 minutes in 350° oven.

FILLING
3 large packages (8 ounces each) cream cheese
4 eggs, separated
1 cup sugar
2 tablespoons cornstarch
2 cups sour cream
½ cup raspberries, crushed

1. Mix softened cream cheese, egg yolks, sugar, sour cream, and cornstarch and beat until smooth.
2. Fold in raspberries.
3. Beat egg whites until stiff and fold carefully into cheese mixture.
4. Pour into crumb-lined springform pan and bake 50 to 55 minutes in 350° oven.

TOPPING
1 cup sour cream
2 tablespoons sugar
½ teaspoon vanilla

1. Mix sour cream, sugar, and vanilla together and spread gently over top of cake.
2. Return to oven and bake for 5 more minutes.
3. Cool, then top with following raspberry glaze.

GLAZE
1 package (10 ounces) frozen raspberries, thawed
2 tablespoons sugar
1 tablespoon cornstarch

1. Place raspberries in saucepan. Do not drain. Combine sugar and cornstarch; add to berries, and cook over medium heat, stirring constantly until thickened.
2. Cool, then gently spread over sour cream topping. Refrigerate.

BERRY MOUSSE

Serves: 6-8
1¹/₂ quart mold

For this dish you may use blackberries, ollalieberries, boysenberries, blueberries, raspberries, or strawberries.

4 cups berries (1¹/₄ cups purée)
4 tablespoons powdered sugar
1¹/₂ tablespoons (1¹/₂ envelopes) gelatin
2 tablespoons water
1 cup whipping cream
2 egg whites

1. Cook berries until soft, using a minimum of liquid (only 2 to 3 teaspoons of water if fruit is dry).
2. Purée the fruit and add powdered sugar.
3. Measure about 1¹/₄ cups of purée into a bowl.
4. Place the 2 tablespoons water in a small dish. Sprinkle in gelatin. Stand this dish in hot water to dissolve gelatin, stirring once to combine.
5. Pour dissolved gelatin very gently into fruit, stirring constantly. Allow to chill and thicken slightly.
6. Whip cream until firm. Fold into fruit mixture.
7. Beat egg whites until firm but not dry. Fold into fruit mixture.
8. Spoon mixture into a lightly oiled 1¹/₂ quart mold. Chill until set.

BERRY DIPS

A simple but elegant dessert.

1 pint fresh strawberries
Powdered sugar
White wine or champagne

1. Refrigerate strawberries (with hulls) for 1 hour.
2. Sift powdered sugar to remove any lumps.
3. Serve with a compote glass of white wine or champagne and a dish of the powdered sugar. Dip strawberry into the wine, then into the sugar, and then into your mouth. Delicious.

FROZEN CRANBERRY PARFAIT

Serves: 6-8

This can be used as pie filling also.

2 cups fresh or frozen whole cranberries
Grated peel of 1 orange
1/2 peeled fresh orange
1 cup sugar
1 tablespoon (1 envelope) unflavored gelatin
1/4 cup orange juice
1/4 teaspoon salt
2 egg whites
1/4 cup sugar
1/2 cup heavy cream, whipped
1 teaspoon vanilla
Whipped cream for garnish

1. Put cranberries, grated orange peel, and orange half through food chopper.

2. Stir in the cup of sugar.

3. Soften gelatin in 1/4 cup orange juice. Place over hot water to melt. Add to cranberry mixture. Chill until it begins to thicken.

4. Add salt to egg whites; beat until they stand in soft peaks. Beat in the 1/4 cup sugar gradually. Fold into cranberry mixture, along with whipped cream and vanilla.

5. Put in parfait or sherbet glasses, cover, and freeze until firm. Garnish with whipped cream, if desired.

SPARKLING MELON COMPOTE

A happy ending to a beautiful day.

> 1 cantaloupe
> 1/2 honeydew melon
> 1 cup shredded fresh coconut
> 1 pint lime, lemon, or pineapple sherbet
> Ginger ale, chilled

1. Cut melons into balls with melon ball cutter.
2. Alternately place cantaloupe and honeydew balls and shredded coconut in 4 parfait glasses.
3. Top each with a scoop of sherbet, then pour just enough ginger ale over all to give it a little sparkle.

GINGERED PEARS

This is good after a heavy meal.

> 6 ripe pears
> 2 tablespoons fresh lemon juice
> 1 1/2 cups sour cream
> 1 tablespoon honey
> 2 tablespoons Triple Sec liqueur
> 1/4 cup crystallized ginger, cut in slivers
> Garnish as desired

1. Peel, core, and cube pears. To prevent discoloration, sprinkle with lemon juice and toss gently.
2. Mix sour cream, honey, Triple Sec, and ginger.
3. Remove pears from lemon juice and add to sour cream mixture.
4. Chill for 1 to 2 hours. Do not prepare too far ahead of time as pears may get soft.
5. Serve garnished with mint leaves, strawberry slices, or mandarin orange slices—anything to add a spot of color.

DANISH ORANGES

Serves: 8-10
Temperature: 300°
Baking time: 7-8 minutes
* (almonds)*
Cookie sheet
9 inch skillet

> ½ cup slivered almonds, toasted
> 2 cups sugar
> 1 cup water
> 4 large navel oranges
> ½ cup brandy
> 1 cup whipping cream

1. Toast almonds in 300° oven for 7 or 8 minutes. Set aside.
2. In a skillet combine sugar and water. Boil 4 minutes to make a thin syrup. Let cool slightly.
3. Peel oranges and remove all white membranes. Cut each orange into ¼ inch slices, then quarter each slice.
4. Add ¼ cup of the brandy and ¼ cup of the warm syrup to orange quarters.
5. Cut orange zest (peel only, no white) into slivers, add to remaining sugar syrup; boil 5 minutes.
6. Remove peel from syrup with slotted spoon. Spread on wax paper to cool.
7. Whip cream until stiff; fold in one-half of the candied orange peel.
8. Sprinkle orange quarters with remaining ¼ cup of the brandy, fold into the whipped cream mixed with candied orange peel.
9. Spoon into sherbet glasses and sprinkle with the other half of the candied orange peel and the toasted slivered almonds.

For another confection, select perfect, plump berries and dry-freeze them in a single layer. Melt a package of semi-sweet chocolate pieces (6 ounces) in the top of a double boiler. Use a fork to dip each frozen berry individually in the melted chocolate and then onto a foil-lined sheet. Slide these back into the freezer until serving time. The first crisp bite of berry and chocolate is delightful.

DRUNKEN FRUIT

Serves: 10-12

This combination of fresh fruits is delicious served as: a first course for holiday dinners; a salad served with chicken or ham; or a light dessert after a heavy meal.

**2 large grapefruit, pared with white
 membrane removed, then sectioned
1 large ripe pineapple, pared, cored, and
 cut in slices or chunks
3 large navel oranges, pared with white
 membrane removed, then sectioned
⅓ cup orange honey
⅓ cup Cointreau liqueur
2 pints strawberries, washed and stemmed
¼ cup Grand Marnier liqueur**

1. Over a large bowl, catch the juices as you peel and section the fruits.

2. Mix honey with Cointreau and add to fruits and juice. Toss until well mixed. Cover and refrigerate 10 to 12 hours. Stir 3 or 4 times.

3. About 2 hours before serving, combine strawberries and Grand Marnier. Refrigerate 1 hour.

4. Combine strawberries with other fruit mixture. Refrigerate 1 hour longer.

5. Serve the fruit medley with some of the juice in glass dishes.

   NOTE: Any leftover fruit will still be delicious the next day. Other combinations of fresh fruits may be combined, such as: peaches, nectarines, bing cherries, raspberries, apricots, olallieberries, grapes, papaya, and kiwi.

   Kirsch and Triple Sec liqueurs also blend well with fruits.

What says summertime more delectably than strawberries and cream? But don't stop there; here are a number of variations on this favorite topping.

1. Dairy sour cream mixed with brown sugar or maple sugar.
2. Cream cheese blended with sugar and lemon juice.
3. Whipped cream mixed with the liqueur of your choice.
4. Grenadine syrup.
5. Plenty of vanilla sugar.

ORANGE APRICOT SHERBET

Serves: 6-8 (1 quart)
6-8 cup freezer tray or
2 quart casserole

Very refreshing because it's made with fresh fruit.

1 cup light cream
1 cup sugar
³/₄ cup light corn syrup
1 cup fresh apricot purée
1 teaspoon grated orange peel
1 teaspoon grated lemon peel
1 cup fresh orange juice
¹/₄ cup lemon juice
2 egg whites, beaten stiff

1. Scald cream and add sugar and corn syrup. Stir until sugar is dissolved. Cool.

2. Wash, pit, and put enough apricots through a blender or food processor to make 1 cup of purée.

3. Combine apricot purée, orange peel, lemon peel, orange juice, and lemon juice. Add to cream mixture; mix and pour into freezer tray and cover with foil. Freeze until almost firm.

4. Scrape mixture into large, chilled mixing bowl. Beat until light and fluffy. Fold in beaten egg whites.

5. Cover and freeze mixture until firm. One hour before serving stir or beat again; return to freezer until ready to serve.

SUMMERTIME ICE CREAM

Serves: 12-16 (4 quarts)
Gallon-size ice cream freezer

4 eggs
2 cups sugar
4 cups puréed fresh strawberries, peaches,
  or other fruit
1 cup milk
4 cups heavy cream
1 tablespoon vanilla
¹/₂ teaspoon salt

1. Beat eggs; gradually add sugar. Continue to beat until mixture is very stiff.

2. Add fruit, milk, cream, vanilla, and salt; mix thoroughly.

3. Pour into gallon-size freezer can and freeze as directed.

White & Gold Custard

Make baked custard with
1½ c. milk, heated.
4 whites of eggs beaten with ½ c.
cold milk, ⅛ tea salt — 4 tb sugar
Mix with hot milk, put into
buttered cups, surround with hot
water & bake till firm. Cool & unmold.
Make soft custard for sauce with
4 yolks of eggs.
2 tb sugar —
⅛ tsp salt
2 cups hot milk —
Mix & cook over water in
double boiler until like cream,
stirring continually — cinnamon
flavor —

This Steinbeck family custard recipe is in John's mother's handwriting, written into the cookbook she received as a bride. Our revised version is on the following page.

WHITE AND GOLD CUSTARD

Serves: 6
Temperature: 325°
Baking time: 45 minutes

This is a delicate, refreshingly simple dessert, appropriately served in antique sauce dishes or sherbet glasses. The recipe came from John Steinbeck's mother.

4 egg whites
$\frac{1}{2}$ cup cold milk
$\frac{1}{8}$ teaspoon salt
4 tablespoons sugar
$1\frac{1}{2}$ cups hot milk

1. In large mixer bowl, combine egg whites, cold milk, salt, and sugar. Beat until fluffy and fairly stiff.
2. Add hot milk, stir gently, and pour into 6 buttered custard cups.
3. Place in shallow pan; fill pan with hot water to $\frac{1}{2}$ inch depth.
4. Bake for 45 minutes at 325.°
5. Cool and unmold. Serve with golden sauce:

4 egg yolks
2 tablespoons sugar
$\frac{1}{8}$ teaspoon salt
2 cups hot milk
$\frac{1}{2}$ teaspoon vanilla

1. Put egg yolks in top of double boiler; whisk to blend. Add sugar, salt, hot milk, and vanilla, whisking to keep smooth.
2. Cook over hot, not boiling, water, stirring constantly until slightly thickened, like heavy cream.
3. Pour through strainer into pitcher. Chill.
4. Garnish with a strawberry, if desired.

   For variations in flavor: Add 1 tablespoon, or more to taste, Amaretto to sauce and garnish with toasted almonds.

   Add Cointreau to taste and garnish with Mandarin oranges.

215

INDEX

218

221

THE STEINBECK HOUSE COOKBOOK
132 Central Ave.
Salinas, CA 93901

Send me _____ copies of your cookbook at $16.95 per copy,
plus $2.00 postage and handling.

NAME_____
Please Print

STREET_____

CITY_____ STATE_____ZIP CODE_____

All proceeds from the sale of cookbooks go to selected Salinas Valley charities.
California residents add 6% sales tax.

MAKE CHECKS PAYABLE TO THE STEINBECK HOUSE

- -

THE STEINBECK HOUSE COOKBOOK
132 Central Ave.
Salinas, CA 93901

Send me _____ copies of your cookbook at $16.95 per copy,
plus $2.00 postage and handling.

NAME_____
Please Print

STREET_____

CITY_____ STATE_____ZIP CODE_____

All proceeds from the sale of cookbooks go to selected Salinas Valley charities.
California residents add 6% sales tax.

MAKE CHECKS PAYABLE TO THE STEINBECK HOUSE

- -

THE STEINBECK HOUSE COOKBOOK
132 Central Ave.
Salinas, CA 93901

Send me _____ copies of your cookbook at $16.95 per copy,
plus $2.00 postage and handling.

NAME_____
Please Print

STREET_____

CITY_____ STATE_____ZIP CODE_____

All proceeds from the sale of cookbooks go to selected Salinas Valley charities.
California residents add 6% sales tax.

MAKE CHECKS PAYABLE TO THE STEINBECK HOUSE